High Seas and Still Waters
a collection of sermons

Matthew R. Nieman

High Seas and Still Waters
ISBN: Softcover 978-1-946478-90-0
Copyright © 2017 by Matthew R. Nieman

All rights reserved. No part of this book may be reproduced or transmitted in any form or by any means, electronic or mechanical, including photocopying, recording, or by any information storage and retrieval system, without permission in writing from the publisher.

To order additional copies of this book, contact:

Parson's Porch Books
1-423-475-7308
www.parsonsporch.com

Parson's Porch Books is an imprint of **Parson's Porch & Book Publishers** in Cleveland, Tennessee, which has double focus. We focus on the needs of creative writers who need a professional publisher to get their work to market, **&** we also focus on the needs of others by sharing our profits with those who struggle in poverty to meet their basic needs of food, clothing, shelter and safety.

High Seas and Still Waters

Contents

Introduction 9
A Beautiful Branch 11
   Isaiah 11:1-10
God Is Here!! 15
   Luke 2:1-20
High Seas and Still Waters 17
   Isaiah 43:1-7
Everybody Has a Name 20
   John 1:29-42
Invitation and Acceptance 24
   1 Samuel 3:1-10, 19-21
Grace in Abundance 28
   John 2:1-11
Essential Personnel 31
   Matthew 4:12-23
Mandatory Minimums 33
   Micah 6:1-8
What We See 38
   Luke 5:17-26
Discovering the Almighty Beside Us 42
   Psalm 46
A Love That Won't Let Go 45
   Luke 15:1-3, 11b-32
The High Five and Other Healing Touches 50
   Mark 5:25-34

Entries and Exits 54
   Mark 11:1-11
A Step Ahead 58
   Mark 16:1-8
"He's Not Here" 61
   Luke 24:1-12
Where the Graves Are 65
   John 20:1-18
Work and Our Reason for It 68
   Leviticus 19:1-2, 9-18
No More Beans! 71
   Luke 24:13-35
On the Road to Resurrection 75
   Romans 6:1b-11
Passing the Baton 79
   Luke 24:44-53
May I See Some ID, Please? 83
   Romans 5:1-5
God Shed His Grace on Thee 87
   Genesis 22:1-14
To Whom We Belong 90
   Ephesians 1:3-14
What Matters 93
   Matthew 15:10-20
Fundamental Neighborliness 97
   Luke 16:19-31

Tilting Our Ears 100
    Psalm 78:1-4

Triggers of the Holy 104
    John 21:1-14

Having a Little Faith 108
    Luke 17:5-10

At Your Service 112
    Mark 10:46-52

The Hope of Any Preacher or Parent 116
    1 Thessalonians 2:9-13

Introduction

These sermons were culled from the hundreds of sermons I preached over a fifteen-year period at the two churches I have most recently served: First Presbyterian Church in Bellevue, Nebraska, and Farragut Presbyterian Church in Farragut, Tennessee.

Both congregations entrusted me with privilege of leading them in worship each week and allowed me to preach with an overarching emphasis on the power and blessing of God's grace and our opportunity and responsibility to respond with joy and service.

The sermons included here are based on scripture texts from the Revised Common Lectionary and follow the liturgical year, beginning in Advent. It is my hope that they reveal the willingness and eagerness God has to love and care for us, so that the high seas we often face may become still waters.

A Beautiful Branch
Isaiah 11:1-10

One day when I was a kid, my parents, brother, and I were walking through a nursery (not the place for babies but the place where plants and flowers are sold). I recall we did not have any intention that day of purchasing a tree to plant in the front yard of where our summer cabin sits. However, the nursery was having a promotion that day and was giving away little trees to the first few people who came through its doors.

This tree, though, was no bigger than a twig. It was about the width of your finger and probably no longer than a foot. While appreciative of the gesture, I'm sure we later scoffed at the idea that this little thing would have any chance of surviving in the wind and upcoming brutal winters that characterize life on Silver Lake in Iowa.

I'm sure only to amuse his two sons, Dad planted that little thing in the ground between the deck of the house and the tool shed not far from it. It looked merely like a long weed sticking out of the ground. Care would have to be given not to run it over with the lawn mower.

If you drove up to the cabin today, some three decades later, and pulled into the driveway, you'd still see that tree. In fact, you wouldn't be able to miss it. It now towers over that deck, the shed, and most of the front yard—providing much needed shade during the summer heat.

Against all odds, that little twig not only survived the elements, but thrived in that place. It endured heat, cold, wind, and rain. Yet, it grew and grew and became a beautiful tree.

Smiles come to our faces when we're able to see how something or someone so young and tiny has grown into a mature and strong contributor to our world. Maybe it's a tree that started out so small and was never given much chance for survival. Or maybe it's a child in our lives who we have a hard time thinking will ever make it to adulthood.

We all know that kids grow up to become adults. It's happened since the beginning of time, but aren't we filled with amazement when we see somebody whom we remember as being so tiny having become such a grown-up?

Those of you who've been around this church for a while probably remember the kids you used to see in this annual Christmas program. Now, they're in the junior high or high school youth group, or they're recently married, or they now have kids of their own in programs like this.

And to see them now brings smiles to our faces—not only because we're happy they're grown but because of the process that takes place, where a child becomes an adolescent, then a young adult, and then a parent of his or her own children.

That child, now an adult, came from parents who birthed them, nurtured them and who long ago were birthed and nurtured, too.

It is part of the long cycle of life—a cycle that God has always been and continues to be part of.

The prophet Isaiah speaks of it when he refers to the coming Messiah that we all anticipate during this Advent. Isaiah refers to him as "a shoot coming out of the stump of Jesse and a branch growing out of his roots." It is a reminder to us that this Jesus who entered the world did not do so out of thin air but came from a lineage, a family of real people who struggled in faithfulness like we all do.

Isaiah says the spirit of the Lord rested on him—the spirit of wisdom and understanding, the spirit of counsel and might, the spirit of knowledge and fear of the Lord. Interestingly, these are the same words we pray immediately after we have baptized a child in this congregation.

Indeed, we can imagine this child Jesus, having come from this strong family heritage of faith, being blessed by the Holy Spirit in his infancy.

And from his birth, Jesus grows into a young man in ways not unlike the young people in our lives. And for those who saw him at his birth but may have lost track of him for a time, imagine their smiles when they see him again in his adolescence or young adulthood.

As we do now with kids in our lives, those adults must have marveled at just how much Jesus—this shoot from the stump of Jesse—had grown. And they no doubt marveled at more than his physical maturity. They most likely noticed how he had, in Isaiah's words, "delighted in the fear of the Lord, did not judge by what his eyes saw or what his ears heard, and clothed himself with righteousness and faithfulness."

This is the king we await during this season of Advent. And while he has come into our lives already, the full effect of what he intends to bring to this world has still not yet been revealed.

Isaiah talks of that glorious day being one in which the wolf shall live with the lamb, the leopard shall lie down with the kid, the calf and the lion and the fatling together. They will not hurt or destroy…

There are days when we can only imagine that world. We can only imagine there being no such thing as bombs being dropped on a neighboring country, or hostages being taken at gunpoint in a high school classroom, or gun violence erupting at a funeral home during a memorial service—all things that have happened in our world within the last several days.

We long for the day Jesus will bring when peace and harmony do indeed reign over the earth. What a beautiful day it will be! As Isaiah writes, "On that day the root of Jesse shall stand as a signal to the peoples; the nations shall inquire of him, and his dwelling shall be glorious."

In the meantime, we reflect on this beautiful branch, one that started out so small and vulnerable and has grown into one of strength, wisdom, and great compassion. This branch is Jesus, of course—God incarnate. But this beautiful branch is also one of us, who grew out of a baby's body to become a man who changed the world. How he did grow!

This past week, I was in a local bookstore. I went up to the counter to make a purchase, gave my debit card to the clerk, and waited for him to run the sale. Upon looking at me and then looking at my name on the card, he said, "Hastings, right?"

"Yeah, I used to live in Hastings," I said.

"I don't know if you remember, but I was in your youth group there."

"Oh yeah," I said. I was sorry I had to ask him his name. And when he told me, it helped me remember him. He looks different now, of course, but he also looked familiar.

His growth and maturity, his willingness to step up and tell me who he was, made me smile.

Life goes on. We are born from our parents who were born from their parents. We grow and grow up and give birth to our kids. From generation to generation, the life process marches on.

And accompanying us always is a God who lived this life himself—the prince of peace who would grow to become our heavenly king.

God Is Here!!
Luke 2:1-20

One of the most entertaining books you'll ever read is Stuart Sample's and Eric Marshall's *Children's Letters to God*. In the book are some real classics, like this one from a boy named Bruce: "Dear God, please send me a pony. I never asked for anything before… you can look it up." Or there's this one from a girl named Joyce: "Thank you for the baby brother, but what I prayed for was a puppy." Or this from little Larry: "Dear God, Maybe Cain and Abel would not kill each other if they had their own rooms. It works with my brother."

Most of these letters leave us smiling or chuckling. They are innocent and wonderfully and refreshingly honest. Some of them do much more than entertain us. They make us think, and they often are synonymous with the sentiments that we as adults often feel but are less willing to express to God.

Take the case of this letter from young Harriet Anne, who wrote: "Dear God, Are you real? Some people don't believe it. If you are, you'd better do something quick."

We know what Harriet Ann is getting at! We wonder if God is real, if God is here. "Where are you God?" we whisper, or even yell at the top of our lungs. The screams usually come when we yearn for something or somebody to stop the unspeakable suffering that has seeped into our lives.

I've been alarmed by the growing number of home invasions reported in the news. Criminals break down doors of people's homes at any hour of the day to steal from or physically assault their victims. I'm not sure there could be a more frightening scenario to endure.

Who could blame the victims from crying out in these situations, "Lord, if you're real, do something!"

Or for people who are enduring a very tough economy right now and have been laid off for months from their primary job, are living off a limited savings and a couple of low-paying part-time jobs, and still get notices in the mail on a regular basis telling them their utilities are going to be shut off soon, it's no wonder they're asking, "Lord, if you're real, do something!"

The same must be true for residents in third world countries like Afghanistan whose villages are controlled by violent and unforgiving tribal leaders and who see the safety of their children being threatened every day. For these children of God, who dare to express a hint of belief in a higher power, it is fair for them to be asking, "Lord, if you're real, do something!"

The world seeks an answer as to who might cure the lame, rescue the downtrodden, and protect the innocent. We seek that every time we read a headline that indicates a betrayal of human sensibilities. Something must change, we say. Something must happen to put a stop to the madness that is hurting so many human beings in all parts of the globe.

Then we come to Christmas, and the end of the time of expectant waiting has arrived. And we are reminded again that God has done something. And that something is somebody and that somebody rested in a manger in Bethlehem. God has done something, and while pain can never be stamped out, God's answer is, "I am here. I am with you, and I am one of you. I will never forsake you."

In a recent essay by Rev. John Buchanan, published in the Christian Century, he tells of the conversation between Holocaust survivor Elie Wiesel and Francois Mauriac, who wrote an introduction to Wiesel's memoir. In response to Wiesel's question, "Where is God now?"—uttered while watching a young boy being executed by the Nazis—Mauriac said, "And I, who believe that God is love, what answer could I give my young questioner…Did I speak of that other Israeli, his brother, the Crucified, whose cross has conquered the world? Did I affirm that the stumbling block to his faith was the cornerstone of mine and the conformity between the cross and human suffering was in my eyes the key to that improbable mystery?"

In the birth of Jesus, we know the answer to the question, "Where is God now?" God is here. God has done something.

High Seas and Still Waters
Isaiah 43:1-7

Amidst the bone-chilling temperatures and mountains of snow that reside outside our windows, I want you to reflect for a minute on the blessings of summer. Maybe it will, for just a few seconds, serve as a reprieve from the punishing effects of the brutal winter we are enduring.

Think for a moment of your favorite summer memory, your favorite summer pastime, or the most beautiful part of summer for you. Maybe it's a location, a hobby, or an image that has become synonymous with the season.

For many of you, summer is synonymous with water—either the practice of being in the water or being by the water.

Being by and in the lake, was and still is the rite of summer for my family. Others love to be fishing on the water. A friend of mine loves to fly fish and will travel just about anywhere there's a body of water conducive to his passion. Kids today love the fun that comes with water parks like Oceans of Fun in Kansas City. And others of you simply enjoy being next to the water and enjoying its beauty and peacefulness on a calm summer afternoon or evening.

On the other hand, while water can be a great source of fun, relaxation and beauty, it can also be a danger and a threat. The tsunami at Christmastime a few years ago was a stark reminder of that. The larger-than-life waves of the Pacific Ocean ignited by an earthquake at sea destroyed the lives of thousands. The flood waters of the Midwest from a couple summers ago did the same to millions-of-dollars of property. And no doubt, when the temperatures around here finally do rise above freezing, causing the ice to thaw and the snow to melt, there will no doubt be too much water. And some homes and other buildings will be worse off for it.

When it comes to faith, water is a good metaphor both for the comfort and nourishment we find in God and the threats to our faith from the world in which we live.

Luke tells us of John the Baptist and his baptizing ways. "I'm just baptizing with water," John says. "You should be watching for the one who is to come who will baptize with the Holy Spirit."

And after the people gathered at the river and Jesus himself was baptized, the Spirit descended upon Jesus like a dove.

Water—for those gathered at peaceful streams—is what represents the nurturing, life-giving, cleansing nature of the God we worship.

In the gospel of John, Jesus is famously quoted during his encounter with the Samaritan woman at the well as saying, "Whoever drinks the water I give will never thirst. Indeed, the water I give him will become in him a spring of water welling up to eternal life."

What gives us life? Is it the vices we engage in—the gambling we do, the alcohol we drink, the food we consume? Is it the stuff we own—the mansions we build, the luxury cars we drive, the iPhone we communicate with? Is it the behavior we give ourselves license to exhibit—casual sex, punitive gossip, selfish ambition?

Or is what gives us life the living water that Jesus Christ offers—a kind of water that forgives, refreshes, nourishes, energizes, and restores our souls? In the water of baptism, we find all this—in addition to the promise of God to keep us forever in God's care.

Speaking of God's eternal care, water is also a good symbol of the dangers we face in our lives and how God saves us from the high seas.

The prophet Isaiah, in chapter 43, instructs the people of Israel as to how God's protection extends into and through the toughest storms. "When you pass through the waters, I will be with you," God says. "And through the rivers, they shall not overwhelm you."

God is our protector and our rescuer, when the raging waters become too violent and threaten to do us in.

In an April 2013 *Reader's Digest* story by Meera Jagannathan, Joe Welch and his son, Joey, were about to start canoeing in a huge swamp in the Florida Everglades. As Joey stood along the water's edge while his father got the canoe ready, he suddenly slipped along the water's edge and fell in face-first. Joe heard a scream, and when he turned around, he saw his son's right arm caught in the jaws of an alligator.

Joe ran toward his son and into the water. He wrapped his left arm around Joey and used his right arm to hit the alligator's snout as hard as he could. It did no good; the alligator would not let go of Joey.

Joe guided Joey up the embankment, dragging the alligator along with him. A bystander came along and kicked the alligator in the belly while Joe continued to hit it in the head. The alligator finally released Joey and slithered back into the water.

Amazingly, Joey suffered only cuts and bruises and no serious puncture wounds. Said Joey after the ordeal, "Because of my dad, I feel less and less afraid of alligators. He's like my bodyguard."

The boy's father wouldn't let go of him, and such is the nature of our heavenly father. Amidst the rough waters, God won't relent in God's pursuit of us and our well-being.

In both the Luke passage and the Isaiah text today, there's a similar tone or message that God wants to communicate both to Jesus and to the people of Israel. It's a statement of connection. Through the waters of Jesus' baptism and through the rough waters that would ordinarily overwhelm, God says to them all, "You are mine. I love you and with you I am well-pleased."

In the very mobile society in which we live today, where people often come in and out of our lives at a very rapid pace, it's quite possible that we are left to ask, "To whom do I belong?" We often lose touch with people because of broken relationships or relationships that fizzle out for some reason. And it affects our well-being.

In the recent PBS series, "This Emotional Life," they chronicle the research that indicates, not surprisingly, that the happiest people in the world are those who are in relationship with others. Beyond the things we own or the status we hold, what really makes us happy and emotionally healthy is that we have a place in others' lives.

We could certainly contend that the importance of relationships extends to God as well. To be in a relationship with others who love us leads us to enjoy and succeed in the lives we have. God seems to know this, because God has said repeatedly that God wants to be in relationship with us.

You are mine, says God. Through the rough seas of high waters and the peaceful streams of calm waters, God reminds us as to whom we belong. We belong to each other and were meant to be together, but more importantly, we belong to God.

Thanks be to God.

Everybody Has a Name
John 1:29-42

Sometimes you can't help but chuckle at the names parents have given their children or the names people assume when they marry their spouses. Some are rather entertaining.

For example, a dentist was once listed in the telephone directory in the following way: First initial "D" and last name "Kay."

Charles Waggon preferred to go by the nickname "Chuck." So, he became Chuck Waggon.

There is a real doctor by the name of Dr. Frank Bonebreak.

Or there was an anesthesiologist named Dr. Les Payne and an optometrist named Dr. Kent C. Straight.

Then there are names that aren't funny but just have an elegant sound to them: Kiara Danelle, Roxanne Moore, Evelyn Blake, Francesca Mordecai, Colton Hartley, Ethan Hawthorne, Elliott Fontana, Russell Esposito.

Finally, there are names that are just rather simple: James Jones, Shawn Hill, Sue Harris, and Bill Brown.

No matter how funny, elegant, or simple our names are, there is no disputing that each of us was given or assumed a name with a purpose behind it. Every parent carefully thinks of what to name his or her children. And every woman takes time to envision what her new name would become if she married the guy she's dating.

What stands out to me this morning about this passage from John 1 is all the names that are contained in it. First, John the Baptist declares Jesus as the "lamb of God who takes away the sins of the world." Later, two of the disciples describe Jesus as "rabbi" and "Messiah." Those two disciples were named in the passage as well: Andrew, Simon Peter's brother, and Simon son of John, whom Jesus says will be called Cephas (which is translated Peter).

Why does Jesus take time to call out these guys by name? Why is it so important to the passage today that John, the author, put in his gospel the fact that Jesus takes time to rename Simon as Cephas?

We don't know why. We don't know why he renamed him in the first place and why he chose the name Cephas. But Jesus' actions here, along with the other names in the passage, remind us that these were not anonymous characters who were in the gospel story. They were real people with real names who, as it turned out, were invited by Jesus to "come and see" where he was staying and to spend the day with him.

Each of them was unique, each of them had talents, gifts, quirks, and tendencies. Jesus knows this, and he reminds them and all of us of just how special each of us is in the kingdom of God.

And with that very personal connection he had to them, he also invites them into his life.

"Where are you staying?" they ask him as they are following him. "Come and see," he says.

That invitation was a common one on Jesus' part. His life is a series of invitations to come and see: what's he doing, what he's teaching, what he's preaching.

Jesus' words and actions in this passage transcend the generations. They have meaning today. They remind each of us that we, too, have a name and an identity. And that identity matters to him.

This morning, we're baptizing Cameron Jay Ehle into the household of faith. We're not baptizing Cameron, Cameron Jay, or Don and Amber's son. No, we're baptizing Cameron Jay Ehle. That's his name, given to him by his parents and held up as his unique identity.

With that name, of course, comes a unique personality—one filled with likes, dislikes, talents, and skills. And it's one that Jesus knows very well and loves uniquely and passionately.

And just as Jesus calls all of us to come and see what Jesus is all about, so will Jesus be calling Cameron Jay Ehle to discover who he is and the role that Jesus has picked out for him to play during his lifetime.

The invitation Jesus makes to Cameron he also makes to us. Come and see, Jesus says, when they inquire as to where he's staying on this day.

It's also an invitation for us to discover what it is that Christ is calling us to do with the lives we've been given.

As we grow from childhood into adulthood and then into senior adulthood, there are many different roles we play throughout our lives. And there can also be many different jobs or tasks to fulfill as Christ's disciples.

No matter what stage of life, those tasks don't end. They may change, but they don't end.

You may have heard that this year, the first wave of baby boomers will reach the retirement age of 65. Retiring at 65 is a relatively recent phenomenon. For thousands of years, the retirement plan for most senior citizens consisted of working the crops or herding sheep until death or, if you couldn't quite push the plow or keep up with the flock anymore, moving in with the kids who, by law, had to take you in.

In 1870, only 2.5 percent of all Americans lived to age 65. Even as recently as 1900, most Americans died by age 47. So, when the retirement age of 60 was established during the birth of Social Security in the 1930s, not many people enjoyed those great government benefits for more than a few years.

Now, of course, the average life-span of an American is in the mid to upper 70s. This means that folks are retiring from their careers in their early to mid-sixties and will enjoy maybe even two more decades of life thereafter.

The dangerous mindset, then, is to believe that when we retire from our jobs, we can also retire from our calling as disciples. And clearly, this isn't what God has in mind.

There is always work to be done for the kingdom, whether it's pre-retirement or post-retirement. Some of us reach retirement age and think to ourselves, "Well, it's time for the younger generation to take on all these tasks in the church and in the community. I've done my time."

Problem is, the call of Jesus to follow has no expiration date. The work of the kingdom is ours to do whether we're 7 or 70. These newly-retiring baby boomers can begin to reverse the trend of seeing retirement as an end and, instead, teach us how to see it as an opportunity to use newly-found free time and disposable income for kingdom purposes.

Some of the best volunteers we have in our congregation are the newly-retireds. I'm so impressed by how many of you in your post-careers have followed Jesus' call to "come and see" by discovering your calling as a disciple during retirement.

No matter our age, Jesus will always know our names and will always be inviting us to come and see how we can be part of his work in the world.

Tomorrow is a national holiday, Dr. Martin Luther King, Jr. Day. And as I ponder the people who are so faithful in following Jesus' directive to come and see what Christ has in store for us, I think of this man who was always, in a non-violent way, pushing for greater justice in the world. And he did this every day of his life. Until the moment he died, he sought to fulfill the task Christ had set before him.

Christ knew his name, of course, and he knows our names and Cameron's name. And he sets before us jobs to do—no matter our age. For as long as we live, our invitation remains intact.

Invitation and Acceptance
1 Samuel 3:1-10, 19-21

There are certain sounds we have difficulty interpreting. We think we know what they are, but we just can't put our finger on them when we hear them.

People who have lived through tornados are often asked what they sound like. And they have a hard time describing the sound. A freight train barreling down on them is one of the more common comparisons we hear.

I remember the first time I was awakened in the middle of the night by an intermittent beeping sound. It took me a good half hour to pinpoint where it was coming from. It was the smoke detector telling us that the battery needed to be replaced. (Don't they always seem to tell us this in the middle of the night?)

And then there are sounds whose origins we can trace but represent a markedly different sound than normal.

I'll never forget the early weekday morning at our house a few years ago. Jenni had gone down to the basement and an audible scream followed her. I know her usual scream—that which indicates the presence of a spider or a malfunctioning washing machine that has left a large pool of water on the floor. This was different on this morning, however. It was a lower-pitched sound, more like an audible gasp.

What she thought was a brown extension cord running along the baseboard of the wall was really a skinny, brown snake. I could just tell that something was different.

From where is that sound coming and what does it mean? These are questions that the boy Samuel evidently had running through his mind when he heard a sound, the sound of a voice calling him late one night.

"I'm here," he said. The problem was that he thought it was somebody else's voice. He thought it had come from his wise, old mentor, Eli.

"No, I didn't call you," Eli said. "Go on back to bed."

This happened a couple more times—a voice calling him and Samuel running to Eli, convinced it was him trying to get his attention.

Finally, Eli—the faithful, old sage—deciphers that it is the voice of God calling this young boy. "When you hear it summoning you, say, 'Speak, Lord. Your servant is listening.'"

And so, the voice spoke again, summoning him by name. "Samuel. Samuel!" And Samuel responds with recognition and confidence. "Speak Lord. Your servant is listening."

It's a call and response between God and an unsuspecting party.

The interplay between God and people least likely to be called upon is found frequently throughout Biblical history. God called the boy Samuel, the boy David, and he called a young girl to carry God's son, Jesus.

Whether it's a young kid, a man or woman, young or old, rich or poor, the conversation is somewhat unlikely. And for those of us who consider ourselves not terribly worthy of receiving such a call, a reflection on the cast of characters God called for special work must certainly leave us confident that God might just be interested in using us for something important.

In Samuel's case, he had the unenviable job of telling Eli where he had gone wrong in his life. He didn't call on a skilled mediator or counselor for this. He didn't want somebody with great experience and a lifetime of wisdom. He called a boy, because it was the boy that Eli knew and who Eli believed and trusted.

Today, we celebrate the good folks in our church family who have answered God's call to lead us on the Session for the next three years. Unlike Samuel, the call came to each of these ruling elders through the voice of the Nominating Committee as adults, full of wisdom and experience. And the gifts they bring will lead us on this journey we are on together—full of adventure and new-found blessing that comes with being diligent and faithful.

And their answering of these calls can also remind us to be on the lookout for the sounds by which God is speaking to us. We all, created in the image of God, have a place and role to play. Whether we are 8 or 80, the call comes through voices that we might not quite recognize.

And let's not forget what comes before our answer. Before we can answer the call, the call must come. And we don't call ourselves. God is the one who first calls us.

God does everything first. He created us first, he loved us before we could love others, and he showed his love through the life, death, and resurrection of Jesus Christ.

God did all this without us having to beckon God for it. God did it all on God's own. Without God acting, we would have no call to answer.

That takes the pressure off. No sense wasting our energy in doing something that God isn't calling us to do. Which means: let's take seriously the process that goes into figuring out how authentic our call is.

Samuel went to Eli at least three times to figure out where his call was coming from. He went to Eli to help him ratify it. He didn't try to figure it out by himself. Only after repeated trips to Eli is Eli able to help him see that it was God who was calling.

This is a story about being summoned, answering the summons, and the strange and wonderful work that goes into determining whether this call is legitimate.

Six or seven months ago, Jenni and I were wrestling with whether God was calling us. We had been beginning to think so, but only when faced with the invitation by the PNC of Farragut Presbyterian Church were we really forced to mightily struggle with whether God's voice was the one we were hearing.

After our visit here with the PNC in April and their offer to us to come and live and work among you, we got back to Nebraska. And I had this huge pit in my stomach for the next two days. Uncertainty.

The next day was Sunday, and I went to the church in Bellevue early as I had always done. And I walked into the building—my workplace and spiritual home for the last twelve years. And it was at that moment that I sensed the voices of the PNC here were indeed the voice of God calling us to East Tennessee, a new home.

As Jenni and I lay in bed that evening, she said, "So, what are you thinking?" And I said, "How well do you speak Southern?" Actually, I said, "It's time to go."

The call came through so many voices. And through those voices, God was calling our names.

Ministers have not cornered the market on good call stories. We take it seriously, but so do all of you. In your wrestling with whether to take this job or that, to retire or not, to move closer to family or not, to parent your children in this way or that, to get involved in this particular ministry or that, listen to the voices in your lives. It may turn out that they are God's voice.

And in case the call doesn't end up being that of God and wrong decisions are made, it's okay. Because the sovereign and all-loving God remains.

Those noises we hear, the ones that seem to be calling our names, can be puzzling. It's always good to see where they are coming from.

Grace in Abundance
John 2:1-11

Today's passage from John 2 is one of those stories that's just plain interesting and fun.

The setting is a wedding feast in Cana. Now mind you, weddings in that day and age were not events over just one afternoon or evening. They usually ran for an entire week. It was a multi-day celebration. And these celebrations were not absent of some serious fun.

Jesus, his disciples, and Jesus' mother had been invited to the wedding on what is perceived to be one of the last days of the celebration. Jesus, by this time, is an adult. Now, guys, imagine going to a wedding with your mother. You've got your buddies alongside you and your mother is present, too. Maybe you're the kind of son who feels he can totally be himself around his mom no matter the occasion. Or, maybe you feel your mom tends to cramp your style once in a while—maybe she has a tendency to brag about her boy or display her expectations of her son wherever she is.

In the opening verses of this passage, we get a sense that Mary knows that her son is a unique guy—that he has the ability to come to the rescue in ways nobody else could.

This is what the text says: "When the wine gave out, Jesus' mother said to him, 'They have no wine.'" Mary seemed to believe that it was possible for Jesus to find a solution to this problem. Maybe she even believed he had the ability to perform a miracle. Her comment makes us wonder what he had revealed to her up to that point that would cause her to believe that such a miracle was possible from him.

Anyway, Jesus' reaction to Mary's comment seems to be a mixture of embarrassment and annoyance. He turns to her and says, "Woman, what concern is that to you and to me? My hour has not yet come."

It's almost as if Jesus didn't want his proud mother to call attention to him. He almost seems content to sit on the sideline. Like a preacher who would just as soon not say the table grace at his or her family's holiday meal, Jesus seems content to just sit back and be a guest.

But Mary doesn't give in. She says to the servants, "Do whatever he tells you." At this point, we can almost hear Jesus sigh and give in. What ensues is miraculous.

As I mentioned, most of these weddings went on for days. Much of that fun was accelerated by the indulging of wine. Wine was part of every such celebration, and it was enjoyed in abundance.

A problem arose, however; they ran out of it. And Jesus concedes to get involved, thanks to the prodding of his mother. Six stone jars, each capable of holding 20 or 30 gallons, were empty. Jesus instructs them to fill them with water. And after they are full, some of what's inside is drawn out to give to the chief steward to taste. They discover the water has become wine.

So now there is an abundance of wine to go around—as much as maybe 180 gallons all together. And not only is there a tremendous amount of wine, it's very good wine. It wasn't what the guests were expecting.

In the gospel of John, Jesus' miracles really aren't referred to as miracles. They are referred to as signs. In other words, the miracle itself is not really what we are supposed to see, as miraculous as it is. The miracle's primary purpose is to reveal to us who Jesus is. And in his turning of the water into wine, we have revealed to us the depths of God's grace.

The first lesson we learn from this sign is that Jesus is all about change or transformation. The simple but miraculous act of turning the water into wine reinforces this reality.

Jesus makes the ordinary holy. Why? That we may celebrate his presence, his reality, his grace-filled nature. That we may gather in joy-filled community because of his presence.

How many of us haven't been caught off guard at times by an interruption of the holy? Amid an ordinary moment, God intervenes and makes it a holy moment. Maybe it was a conversation with one of our children that started out so routine but ended in unforgettable connection.

This past week, our youngest son, Joey, was having a rather routine day—full of highs and lows. When I picked him up at the babysitter in the afternoon, he had just run into a bed and hurt himself across his chest. There were tears and then the "boo-boo bag" to place on it and make it feel better. We got into the car to go pick up Jacob from school, and as we parked the van and got out, Joey wacked himself across the forehead with his seatbelt. And the tears started again. And through these tears, in a tone of desperation and despair, he says, "Why do I keep hurting myself?"

And while I wanted to say to him, "Because you're five and most five-year-olds are clumsy and you should just be more careful," his sense of helplessness and resignation could only engender a hug and consolation from his dad.

In that embrace came a holy moment. Jesus changes the ordinary into the extraordinary.

The second sign we get from Jesus in this miracle is the sheer scope of God's grace. It is abundant, and it is the best.

Jesus takes ordinary water and turns it into gallons and gallons of the best wine. Not only in terms of volume but in terms of quality, God's grace is abundantly provided. And despite his mother's prompting, we'll assume he chose to perform this sign not out of obligation to any who were at the wedding but because he desired for all to have a good time, for all to celebrate, and for the celebration to be the best.

This is the nature of God's grace. It is not reserved for just those who arrived at the party early, it is not watered down, and it is not scarce. It is for all, it is abundant, and it is 100% filled with love and joy.

We too often minimize the breadth and depth of God's grace. We receive it in portions based on a scale of our own merits. ("Ah, probably not due for much grace today. My behavior at that morning meaning sabotaged that." Or, "Ah, probably can't count on God's grace anymore. My ignorance of God's presence for all those years I'm sure disqualifies me." Or, "Ah, probably not going to get the same kind of grace *she's* getting from God. I'm just not as 'all in' as she is when it comes to being a disciple.")

If there's anything we learn from this joyful tale of water becoming wine, it's that Christ can interject at any moment a full dose of grace for any of us. At the drop of a hat, love, reconciliation, and forgiveness reign down on all of us.

The guests at that wedding were amazed at what he had done. They would never forget that moment. They would be changed forever.

In that wonderful change that took place, the party roared again. Abundance overcame scarcity, and they celebrated.

We're invited to the party, too.

Essential Personnel
Matthew 4:12-23

The phrase is a familiar one. When budget talks collapse and the government shuts down, this is the phrase that is trotted out. When the earth suddenly quakes under the people of California, often a certain segment of people is called out while the rest are told to stay home. When tornadoes blow through the Midwest and disrupt everything in their course, only certain people should risk the dangers involved. And when snowstorms hit, crippling transportation systems, these are the folks who must make it into work.

These are maintenance people, road crews, ambulance drivers, fire fighters, electric and gas company workers, truck drivers, and a whole host of service people who are taken for granted when things are running smoothly.

We call them "essential personnel."

Think about that phrase. Think about what it means to be essential personnel. Then, if you want to be humbled, think about what it is like to be non-essential personnel. We are the ones who are told to not bother coming in to work during a winter blizzard. Consider the fact that the world can go on without some of us.

The good news is that in God's eyes we are all essential personnel. As essential personnel, we are loved and forgiven, cleansed by the waters of baptism, and promised new life. And as part of our essential-ness, we are also called to do some important work.

As Jesus walked by the sea of Galilee, he noticed some essential personnel. He saw a couple of brothers named Peter and Andrew. They were working, performing the difficult tasks that come with fishing. Jesus said to them, "Follow me and I will make you fish for people."

Peter and Andrew weren't fishing just to kill some time on a beautiful day. No, they were fishing because it was how they made a living. They needed to fish. For their own survival, they needed to be throwing those nets into the water again and again.

But, they were essential personnel to Jesus. He went to them—not the ones who necessarily had the most influence in their community, not the ones who had the most resources, and certainly not the ones who were the most sophisticated. He sought them out because he valued them as much as anybody else. And he had a role for them to play in this revolution he was embarking upon.

The kingdom of God could not operate without them. So, upon his calling them, they left their nets and followed Jesus.

We can see ourselves in the eyes of Peter and Andrew. We are ordinary people, too, who do our jobs the best we can with the talents that have been given us. If we're not careful, we might be lulled into believing we are non-essential—non-essential to the thriving and success of the world. And worse yet, we might believe we don't matter—that God surely has more important people picked out for the transformation of the world.

And then we hear this story of the fishermen being tapped on the shoulder by Jesus and called to follow, and we draw the connection between the disciples and ourselves: "If they can be followers of Jesus, so can we."

We have what it takes, as much as these long-ago fishermen did. We are highly valued by Christ and therefore have an important role to play.

The best indicator of our commitment to this role of following is how willing we are to turn our attention away from our own interests and focus instead on the interests of others. Just like the disciples, we are called to take up a second career. Aside from our jobs and interest in making ourselves happy, we are called to turn our energy to those around us so that they too can be blessed with the love of Jesus Christ.

This is especially what makes us essential.

By taking on a second career as Jesus' fishers of people, we too will find Jesus, in the toil, the conflicts, the sufferings, the challenges, and the unknown through which we shall pass. And along the way, those who see our light might just have the light of Christ burning in them too.

We are all essential personnel in this very important work. Thanks be to God for Christ's calling, challenge, and the rewards that witnessing brings to our lives.

Mandatory Minimums
Micah 6:1-8

When you hear the term "greatness," maybe you think about all those individuals, companies, teams, or cities that have achieved the pinnacle of success. I'm hoping the Atlanta Falcons, after what they did to my Green Bay Packers last Sunday, can achieve greatness against the Patriots next Sunday.

As an indication of our human quest to be the best, we long for greatness—not only in ourselves but in the organizations, we're a part of or root for. In fact, there are all kinds of tools out there to help us achieve greatness.

Some of you may be familiar with the 2001 bestselling book *Good to Great: Why Some Companies Make the Leap and Others Don't* by Jim Collins. Collins conducted research on 11 companies that he said had made the leap from good to great. And not only did other company CEOs gobble up the book in search of the recipe for greatness for their organizations, but so did church leaders.

Collins described greatness as having a "distinctive impact" and "superior performance" shepherded by what he called a "level 5" leader, somebody who was completely off the charts when it came to getting their organizations to achieve.

We adopt greatness language in the church too. We often think that the measure of a church's greatness is in how distinctive our impact is and how measurable its performance is in all the metrics that businesses use: how bigger, how stronger, how richer, and how famous we become.

It's worth noting that of the 11 "great" companies that Collins identified 16 years ago, most of them are not so great a decade and a half later.

Circuit City was one of the companies. The electronics retailer went out of business in 2009.

Fannie Mae, the federal mortgage lender, had to be bailed out by the government during the mortgage crisis of 2009.

Gillette, another of the companies, was sold.

And five of the companies—Abbott Labs, Kimberly-Clark, Kroger, Walgreens, and Wells Fargo—have done okay but with only modest market gains.

This all reinforces how difficult it is to sustain greatness. Past results do not predict future performance.

And it does raise the question of whether greatness is really the best goal for an organization—a business, a municipality, a country, or even a church.

Micah wrote to the nation of Israel during a time when it had slipped from greatness and found itself under the control of the Assyrian empire. It was a shadow of its former self. The kingdom had reached its heights during the rule of David and Solomon but had now found itself conquered and divided.

Micah chronicles how the nation had gone off the rails by oppressing the poor, corruption in its government, a loss of order, and greed amongst its officials.

And Micah delivers a message of judgement on the nation, condemning them for what they had done and who they had become. But as always happens with God, despite the judgement there is always hope. God tells them they will be restored. The question is how it would happen.

Initially, the people consider all those familiar rituals to get them back into a state of greatness. They believe it's their deeds that will earn them favor. Micah asks, "Shall we come before the Lord with burnt offerings? With calves a year old? Will the Lord be pleased with thousands of rams and ten thousand rivers of oil?" Surely this is how they will achieve greatness in God's eyes.

These are similar questions we in the church today might ask as we attempt to become great churches or attempt to reestablish the greatness we think we have lost over time. With what shall we come before the Lord? Shall it be spectacular cathedrals? Shall it be rising budgets? Shall it be all the seats filled on Sundays? Is this how God will truly bless us—if we do all these things that we think will make us great?

Our church's facility here is in solid shape. It is beautiful by many accounts. But it's not a cathedral. It has parts that none of us would qualify as beautiful. Nor does it seat thousands. Our membership is stable, but that's only after a steady decline from the church's peak a decade or so ago.

By these measures, we haven't achieved greatness if we had wanted to.

But if we read Micah a little more in chapter 6, we learn from him that maybe God doesn't want us to be great according to these measures. Instead, maybe God desires for us to simply be good.

Micah says, "He has told you, O mortal, what is *good*." What does the Lord require? Goodness, not greatness. And it comes in the form of how we relate to one another and to God.

Here, Micah outlines how our goodness is measured. It's measured in three ways. First, God through Micah calls us to "do justice." The Hebrew word for justice refers to God's order for all of life. So, to do justice means that we order our lives, including our interactions with others, in accordance with God's will. And that means providing equality for all, ensuring all people are treated with dignity and respect no matter their background or their circumstance.

And of course, we don't hear from Micah the phrase "*speak* words of justice." No, the words are "*do* justice." There is action he calls the people of Israel to. And it's not about religious ritual; it's about how they should treat their fellow human beings. Work for, seek, *do* justice. This is what the Lord desired from them and desires from us.

The second way to goodness involves loving kindness. Being kind to each other isn't necessarily a way to become great at anything. But it's a key ingredient of the goodness that God seeks from all of us. To love, to be kind to each other—in cases where we agree with each other and have much in common, but also in cases where we don't see eye to eye or share common interests or even values—this is the mark of goodness in God's eyes.

And the third component of the goodness formula is to walk humbly with God. People of faith (and even people of no faith) find goodness when they don't make themselves bigger than God. And how many times do we easily slip into a mode of thinking or feeling that ranks *our* interests as most important compared with those of our family members, co-workers, or those in the other communities of which we are a part?

Being humble—again, not a necessity for greatness; but it's a key ingredient to finding goodness.

This past Thursday night, the furnace at our house went out. And so the next day, two technicians from a local heating and air company came by to fix the problem. Their names were Charlie and Marcus, a couple of younger guys. And as soon as they had met me, they were eager to teach me the intricacies of how furnaces work.

Has this ever happened to you? You got a problem, you call somebody to come and fix the problem, and you get a tutorial on plumbing systems, air conditioners, furnaces, car engines, or electrical systems. And you really don't desire such a tutorial; you just want them to fix the problem. But they must convince you, they think, that they know what they're doing. So, they tell you about compressors and motors and coils and condensation and valves and how air moves and where it moves.

As Charlie was explaining all this, I nodded my head like I had a clue what he was talking about. And Charlie, bless his heart, kept talking and talking. He loved and took great pride in his work.

Two and half hours after they arrived, Charlie and Marcus were done. Charlie was writing up the ticket, so I could pay him. Only $89 for the service call.

I was feeling pretty good about the simple and inexpensive fix, so because of that and because these guys were really nice to deal with, I offered each of them a cold soda on their way out. Charlie gladly accepted; but Marcus declined graciously. And he said, "Thanks but I've still got some hot coffee out in my thermos from early this morning."

Really. Marcus chose day-old coffee over a fresh cold soda late in the day. Maybe he didn't care for soda; or maybe his choice was a reflection of something deeper. Marcus was clearly Charlie's assistant, but he was very knowledgeable, very endearing, and very committed. He had talked of a young family at home, and he clearly was a hard-working guy who was simply trying to live a good life. That doesn't mean he isn't striving for some sort of professional or personal greatness, but one just had the feeling he was committed to goodness. Hot coffee, still in the thermos, still good eight hours later.

Micah says, "He has told you what is good. And what does the Lord require, but to do justice, love kindness, and walk humbly with our God."

Weeks ago in my planning, I had titled this sermon "Mandatory Minimums." And the rationale then was that these requirements of living were the least that we should do for God in response to God's goodness upon us. They should be where we start in our discipleship and build from there.

But now, I would have changed the title. Instead, it should be "Mandatory Maximums." Because maybe this is all that the Lord requires from us. Maybe the Lord only wants us to be good and doesn't care as much about our being great. Because goodness is about a way of living, a way of interacting with God and with one another. And maybe that's where our lasting peace and happiness dwell.

What We See
Luke 5:17-26

Preached at the stated meeting of the Presbytery of Missouri River Valley

Last November, in preparation for the role I've assumed here this morning, I attended the national presbytery moderators' conference in Louisville. There were about 130 incoming moderators from around the country who were there to brush up on their parliamentary procedure and leadership skills in advance of our upcoming year as leaders of our presbyteries.

As we had conversation among us, we also assessed the state of our denomination and each of us commented on the state of our presbyteries. And as you might expect, much of the discussion focused on what was not going well.

There were laments about declining membership, church attendance, and volunteer activity. And there was an overall concern about the ongoing marginalization of the church throughout our society and culture.

Also at this conference, we were shown a 10-minute video entitled "Seeing Red Cars." It's narrated by Laura Goodrich, a life coach and consultant. And in the video, this is what she says:

"Through my work as a coach and advisor, I've learned something important: we get more of what we're focused on. I call it, seeing red cars.

"Say you recently bought your dream car. Custom wheels, full chrome bumpers, and it's red. Driving it home for the first time, you start to notice something: It seems like there's a lot of red cars out there. The next day, what do you notice? There are definitely more red cars on the road. By the end of the first week, you're thinking, 'Is everyone driving a red car?'

"You're seeing red cars because that's what you're focused on.

"Who's putting all those thoughts of red cars in our heads? We are because that's what we're focused on."

We tend to focus only on those things we see. And in the life of the church today, specifically our denomination, the things we see aren't that pleasant.

There's declining attendance, an aging membership, disagreements over theology and authority of scripture, the marginalization of the church in our society, and on and on.

These are big barriers to ministry. At least, that's how we see them. And when all we see are these barriers and obstacles, our vision gets tainted with doubt and discouragement.

At our church in Bellevue, we've welcomed 10 new adults and their four children into our membership in the last month. Four of those adults are two young couples without any children, and four others are young adults with kids.

That's a pretty good month for us; in fact, today when young adults are wary of joining any kind of established institution, that's a pretty good month for any church or service organization.

It's something our leadership should be celebrating. But guess what happened at our Membership Committee meeting last week? All we could do, it seems, was lament. We were concerned about how well we'd be able to assimilate these new members into our ministry. There was also concern that we didn't get all of these new folks to the same two orientations we had offered over the last month.

By the sound of the conversation, it was as if we had deleted 10 from the membership roll instead of adding 10.

When we only see barriers and threats, that's all we focus on.

In Luke 5, the friends of this paralyzed man saw the potential of Jesus to heal their friend. And so, they decided they would take him to see Jesus. But they were quickly confronted with a barrier. A large crowd had gathered around the house where Jesus was teaching. And in doing so, they would prevent these loyal friends from getting to Jesus with their disabled friend.

The thing about these friends, though, is that this barrier didn't cloud their vision. What they saw was not discouragement and defeat. While certainly a challenge for them, the crowd blocking their path to Jesus was simply a curve in the road to their ultimate destination—a destination they would not be denied.

They went up on the roof and lowered their friend in his bed down through the tiles right in front of Jesus.

In seeing the faith these friends had, he said to the paralyzed man, "Your sins are forgiven," and later, "stand up and take your bed and go home."

These guys refused to be held back. Defeat and obstacle weren't in their line of sight. They only saw possibility at the feet of Jesus.

In the church today, sure, we must be realistic. Maybe we shouldn't look at everything through rose-colored glasses. Perhaps the reality of our situation as a presbytery and as congregations doesn't permit it.

But we still have the option of choosing what it is we see, choosing what it is we're going to focus on. It can be more than just challenges and obstacles. If we choose, we can see something different.

In our presbytery, we can choose to focus on the possibilities for transformation and we can choose to focus more on what unites us than what divides us.

It's about what we see.

I once heard Dr. Tom Long, of our denomination's finest preachers, tell of his experience one day at a conference he was attending in Boston.

The conference was not one he had been looking forward to. It was one where scholars like him got together to listen to each other deliver their academic papers. And so, as he was sitting there, his heart just wasn't into it. So, he got up and walked out of the room and outside of the hotel to get some fresh air. He decided to go for a walk.

Across the street from the hotel in downtown Boston was one of the old historic churches of the city. And so Long walked on over to it and just wondered if the front door might be open. Sure enough, it was unlocked.

Long entered through that big old wooden door and when he got inside he was graced by the sight of that grand gothic sanctuary—one that reflected the omnipotence and protection offered by a loving God. Needing a moment for reflection, he stepped inside the worship space and stood quietly for a few moments.

Suddenly, he heard this booming voice singing, "Now Thank We All Our God with hearts and hands and voices."

Long gazed across the cavernous room but didn't see anybody in the chancel that would've offered up such a rendition of the familiar hymn.

"Who wondrous things hath done, in whom this world rejoices." He couldn't figure out from where this voice was coming. So, he had to search for it.

He started walking down the aisle. And as he walked closer to the front of that sanctuary and in hearing that voice grow louder singing those words of praise and thanks, he finally discovered the responsible party.

He looked down and saw a man lying flat on his back. It was the custodian of the church polishing the undersides of those historic church pews.

Even in the monotony and isolation of his work, this man saw the blessings of God and chose to give thanks.

It's important to take inventory of what we see. Are our eyes trained only on the injustices, tragedies, and unfairness of our lives? Or do we see blessing and realize that these blessings are served up by a God who sees us and offers us gifts we don't deserve?

The words of 13th century poet Fra Angelico are fitting:

"The gloom of the world is but a shadow behind it. Yet within reach is joy. There is radiance and glory in the darkness could we but see. And to see, we have only to look."

Discovering the Almighty Beside Us
Psalm 46

Last Saturday, Jenni and I were on the golf course in Mesa, Arizona. It was a beautiful day—mid 70s and sunshine. And we got paired up with another guy who was out playing. He was probably in his late 40s or early 50s and he divides his time between his winter home in Arizona and his summer home in Vancouver.

He was very nice, but we noticed he wasn't shy about complaining about the group in front of us that was slowing us down a bit. We ended up waiting on the tee or in the fairway while the four guys ahead of us lined up their putts and took their practice strokes before finally hitting their ball.

Our playing partner seemed to grow more and more impatient, claiming, "They're really not very good golfers anyway; I don't know why they're taking so much time."

Jenni and I, on the other hand, could not have cared less about the slow play. Here we were, having just gotten off a plane from snowy and cold Nebraska a few hours earlier, basking in the sun, with no wind, our feet resting on green grass, and having earlier applied sunscreen to prevent burning—in January!

It could have taken us all day to play those eighteen holes and we wouldn't have cared. At one point, as I was standing in the fairway (one of the few times my ball landed in the fairway), I turned to her and remarked how it doesn't get much better than this. It was one of those moments where we couldn't help but be still and know that God is near.

What a wonderful moment—in the beauty of the earth, the celebration of a pretty day—to know without a shadow of a doubt that God is near. We've all had these moments, many of them. They are the mountaintop moments—a relaxing vacation, a new marriage, a birth in the family, the joy of a completed project at work, the winning of a gold medal if you're an Olympic athlete. Life is good, and God is near.

But we all know that life isn't all about mountaintop moments. As life happenings go, they are unfortunately the minority. Life for the most part is consumed by ordinary moments that happen again and again and again.

Every weekday morning, our household has a routine (as I'm guessing your household does). The alarm goes off at 5:30 and Jenni is on the treadmill. I'm in the shower by 6:15 and dressed by 6:45 when I get our oldest son out of bed. He has his breakfast at 7, Joey is up by 7:20, they change their clothes and brush their teeth at 7:30, and we're out the door at 7:40 so that Jacob is at school by 8:00.

On many days, as I'm completing my tasks to hit all those target times, I say to myself, "This is a Groundhog Day moment." The movie *Groundhog Day* from several years ago was about a guy waking up to the same situation day after day. It never changed.

If I didn't wear different clothes each day of the week, I might think the same morning was repeating itself. Because it's all the same. The lunch I make for Jake is the same every day, the struggle I go through to get the boys' clothes and coats on and get out the door every day is the same, the drive to the babysitter and the school is the same, the commercials on the radio stations we listen to happen at the exact same time every day.

It's such a routine. And while routine can be a very good thing, you get to wondering, "What's this all about or what's the point of it all?"

It's in those routine moments, those ordinary moments, where it is especially critical that we pause—either physically or mentally. It is important that we, in some way, are still and realize that the God who created us is near. When we do that, we more fully comprehend that even though our days are routine and ordinary and even boring at times, each one of them is precious and is a blessing.

It's easy to be still and acknowledge God's presence on the mountaintop, and it takes a little more discipline during the ordinariness of life. But it gets real hard to do this during tough times. Yet the essence of faith is when we acknowledge what the Psalmist does: During life's bleakest moments, "God is our refuge and strength, an ever-present help in trouble."

That is the epitome of faith: as the ship is sinking, so to speak, acknowledging God's presence and willing assistance is no small affirmation.

In the book, *Holy Adventure*, our Lenten study for this year, Bruce Epperly speaks of Martin Luther King, Jr. In one of his sermons, King "told of discovering God in the midst of the darkest night of the spirit. During the first days of the Montgomery, Alabama, bus boycott, King received an anonymous, life-threatening phone call. Trembling with fear and unable to sleep, King went downstairs to make a cup of coffee. As the coffee perked, he poured out his soul to God: 'I am here taking a stand for what I believe is right. But now I am afraid. The people are looking to me for leadership, and if I stand before them without strength and courage, they too will falter. I am at the end of my powers. I have nothing left. I've come to the point where I can't face it alone.' In that moment, King felt a quiet presence that would forever change his life. An inner voice whispered, 'Stand up for righteousness, stand up for truth. God will be at your side forever.' Although there was no promise that he would escape trouble, King recalled, 'My uncertainty disappeared. I was ready to face anything. The outer situation remained the same, but God had given me inner calm.'"

Amid death threats and other persecution, King was able to be still and know that God was near.

So, no matter the days—joyful and beautiful days, routine days, or scary and uncertain days—people of faith call on the name of the Lord. To be able to do so with confidence no matter the emotion or stage of life is a sign of our complete dependence on a God who creates, protects, saves, and redeems.

Another season of Lent has begun. Lent is a time for repentance and self-examination. It's a time for strengthening our relationship with the God who truly is near to us. It's a time for acknowledging those moments, no matter our mood or our life stage, where God is near. Maybe it's in the hug you give your spouse or partner, maybe it's the time you take to play with your kids, or maybe it's the time you take to volunteer for your church or other favorite charity.

Lent is the time to be still and to discover the Almighty beside us.

A Love That Won't Let Go
Luke 15:1-3, 11b-32

At the condo complex where my mother and father spend a couple of months each winter, there is a weekly tradition that occurs outdoors there every Wednesday evening. It is the weekly patio party. From 5 to 7 p.m., the residents gather there for drinks, appetizers, and conversation. It is open to everybody who lives at the complex. There is a standing invitation: Everyone who takes up residence there—whether they are permanent residents or winter snowbirds—is welcome and encouraged to attend.

It makes no difference whether you are there in retirement mode or still working, whether you are escaping cold, Midwestern winters or are Arizona natives. Everyone is welcome at the weekly patio party. And my mom and dad often remark about the people they meet there each year and with whom they establish relationships over a period of just several weeks.

It's nice that an invitation to a party doesn't depend on one's status or background.

Tom Long, in his book *Shepherds and Bathrobes*, says: "I was once staying in a motel in a large city and was surprised to find, posted to the elevator door, a small, handwritten notice that read, 'Party Tonight! Room 210. 8:00 p.m. Everyone invited!' I could hardly picture who would throw such a party, or for what reason.

"Alas, the sign by the elevator soon came down, replaced by a typewritten statement from the motel staff explaining that the original notice was a hoax, a practical joke. That made sense, of course, but in a way it was too bad. For a brief moment, those of us staying at the motel were tantalized by the possibility that there just might be a party going on somewhere to which we were all invited – a party where it didn't make much difference who we were when we walked in the door, or what motivated us to come; a party we could come to out of boredom, loneliness, curiosity, responsibility, eagerness to be in fellowship, or simply out of a desire to come and see what was happening; a party where it didn't matter nearly as much what got us in the door, as what would happen to us after we arrived."

Here in Luke 15, in the famous Parable of the Prodigal Son, a dad is throwing a party. And everyone is invited, including both a son who has squandered his share of his father's money and another son who just can't believe his father would be so gracious to his wayward brother.

The question may rightfully be asked: In which of these characters do we see ourselves?

Do we see glimpses of ourselves in this young kid who had to escape his parents and make out on his own, tired of being tethered to a demanding father who seemed to want to mold him into his own image and not give him any room to live his own life?

Or instead, do we see glimpses of ourselves in the older son—the loyal, faithful, obedient brother who did everything right and resents the fact that his father is throwing a lavish party for his brother, the screw-up?

Or, but not likely, do we see ourselves in the father? This dad, who had worked hard to provide for both his sons, but who had one of them race off with his inheritance and waste it? This dad who nonetheless raced out to meet his home-coming son, who didn't want to hear of any apology but instead only wanted to celebrate the return of his own?

Most of us see ourselves as either option A or B. We are A, the wild child who comes home with our tail between our legs, or B, the one who'd always done everything right and has now gotten the short end of the appreciation stick.

But option C, the dad who's able to overlook the misbehavior of his child and welcome him home with no conditions? Probably not.

For those of us who are parents, we'd like to think we could be that dad. We'd like to think we would not have any concern for what went on when the youngest sewed his wild oats. We'd like to think nothing would have mattered at all except celebrating the kid's return.

But we'd probably be more likely to blend in some celebration with some stipulations: "We're glad you're back home, son, but why don't you go take a shower first and put on some pants that aren't sagging and a shirt that doesn't look like it's sat in the dryer for a week. Get yourself cleaned up, we'll have a nice get-together and then we're going to talk about where you're going to put in your first job application on Monday morning, so that you can start saving for that deposit on an apartment."

As loving as we are, we love conditionally most of the time, with strings attached, with still little bits of disappointment occupying the far corners of our hearts.

The dad in this story, though? His heart contained the purest of loves.

If we were marketing our faith to a skeptical world, what would be the talking points, the key qualities that make our God worth checking out?

If I had to pull out just one story from the New Testament to make our case for the God we worship and serve, it would be this narrative from Luke, because the parable of the Prodigal Son reveals the unmerited, unlimited, unconditional love of God.

What does each human being, no matter their race, nationality, family background, or social status long for? He or she longs to be loved, no matter their success or their failure. We all want to have somebody put their arms around us and tell us how much they love us regardless of what we do or don't do in response.

When the Pharisees and the scribes were grumbling about how Jesus was welcoming sinners and eating with them, he showed them what unconditional mercy is all about when he told them this story of a father who ran to meet his wayward son and before he could utter his words of repentance threw his arms around him and kissed him.

In Christ we have a God who doesn't prevent our sinful ways from blocking his mercy toward us. We should repent, yes. We should commit ourselves to a new way of life without sin, yes. But, in the end, this God whom we worship and serve has mercy on us either way.

Unfortunately, we still place more emphasis on what we do with our lives rather than on what God has done for us in the life of Jesus Christ. Great mercy for an undeserving lot like us, demonstrated in a sacrifice on the cross, speaks volumes to a world in need of great mercy.

Why do we have such a hard time presenting this big picture idea to the world around us? Why do we have such a hard time with the unconditional love of God?

Maybe we fail to trumpet God's extraordinary ability to be merciful because we are so unwilling to be merciful ourselves—

because it's so hard for us to be the father in this story. It is hard to forgive and forget. It's hard to put behind us the hurtful ways of others and simply love them.

Maybe you know the cartoon strip *Calvin and Hobbes*. Calvin is a little boy with an overactive imagination and a stuffed tiger, Hobbes, who comes to life as his imaginary friend. In one cartoon strip, Calvin turns to his friend Hobbes and says, "I feel bad that Susie called me names and hurt my feelings. I wish she wouldn't have done that." Hobbes replies, "Maybe you should forgive her." Calvin thinks about it for a moment and then responds, "I keep hoping there's a less obvious solution."

Like Calvin and like the older brother in Luke, we much rather prefer justice to mercy when we have been hurt by somebody else. Like the older brother, we have worked for what we have, and it's unfair that everyone else should not have to do the same. We have earned God's favor (or so we think) by "staying at home." We have merited his acceptance by the good life that we live. So how dare God receive and accept our sinful brother who has returned home saying he's sorry!

That desire for justice over mercy seems all well and good, however, until we find ourselves on the other side, longing for mercy. And then that's where we reap the same benefits the prodigal enjoyed. We find a God whose mercy supersedes judgment, a God whose arms are outstretched after our missteps and blunders. We find a God who welcomes us back home time and time again.

Dr. Louis Weeks, former president of Union Seminary in Richmond, Virginia, translates Romans 8:28 this way: "We know that to those who experience the love of God, who are filled with yearning for that love to guide and complete their lives—to them it is clear that in all of life's moments, events, and people, God is working for good."

When we experience the love demonstrated by a father to his prodigal son, we can't help but believe God is working in the world for good.

This is an appropriate and necessary message to the world this year, above all those messages about doctrine and Godly living (as much as Jesus wants us to live Godly lives). The world aches for mercy, and to a world more and more skeptical about religion, the unconditional love of God through Jesus Christ must be the message that soars far above all others.

God loves us. Like a loving father, God loves us with a love that will not let us go. Thanks be to God!

The High Five and Other Healing Touches
Mark 5:25-34

Unfortunately, sad stories of sexual misconduct are far too common. And often, misconduct is defined by inappropriate touching.

Harmful and hurtful kinds of touching undermine the beauty and beneficial qualities of healing touch—a kind of touch that Jesus practiced so often during his ministry.

Jesus took Peter's mother-in-law by the hand and cured her debilitating fever. He placed a mixture of saliva and dirt on a blind man's eyes, and man regained his sight. Jesus touched the leper, restoring him in body, mind, spirit, relationships, and social position.

These are just a few of the ways in which Jesus used the power of touch to bring healing and wholeness to the people to whom he ministered.

We, too, can use the power of touch to bring comfort and healing to people's bodies and spirits. Physical therapists, chiropractors, and massage therapists employ such techniques to reduce pain and renew strength in patients' bodies. We comfort each other during times of sadness and consolation by embracing one another in gentle hugs. We share our affection with a spouse or our children through a kiss on the cheek. And we greet one another by the standard handshake.

Touch can also foster unity and camaraderie as well. If you've watched any of the college basketball on television the last few days, you may have noticed—in close games—players on a particular team seated together on the bench. As the games wind down with their team on the verge of winning, players on the bench will often interlock their arms while sitting next to each other as a way of saying, "We need to stick together, we're almost there, our bond is strong."

Indeed, in athletics, touch among teammates is a way of showing support and celebration.

Last week, Sports Illustrated did a story on the origin and meaning of the "high five" and other celebratory acts that have defined success.

Author Chris Ballard writes, "Sometimes a man just can't contain himself: He has to celebrate. And for a certain type of man, that means rearing back, cocking his arm and unleashing a high five of resounding power, a high five that says, 'I'm excited about that which just occurred,' a high five that in its very execution creates a vortex of enthusiasm into which everyone within its vicinity is sucked.

"What is it about the five and its innumerable permutations that grab us so? After all, it is a simple act, one that many two-year-olds learn before they can talk, yet we relish it, embellish it, mock it and bungle it.

"From President George W. Bush's inexplicably chest-bumping an Air Force Academy graduate to the Obamas' much-discussed First Fist-Bump, we are a nation forever trying to find the right way to celebrate, and in no arena is the physical vocabulary richer than in sports."

We touch in a way that brings us together and celebrates our achievements. It can bolster our spirits.

In Jesus' ministry, we so often think of Jesus being the one to instigate touch to create healing. And he does it repeatedly. But in our story from Mark 5 today, we find that Jesus' healing takes place not because of his first reaching out to somebody, but because of somebody reaching out to him.

The woman we read about had been bleeding for 12 years. She was no doubt exhausted and tired from not only being sick but also from being shunned by the people around her. She asserts herself one day by coming up to Jesus, the one she believed would make her well, and reaching out to touch him.

She was immediately healed; and Jesus proclaims, "Your faith has healed you. Be freed from your suffering."

This woman took the initiative to get well. Jesus held the power, but she wasn't shy about doing what she needed to do to get well.

This story doesn't validate the theory that if we just believe in Jesus more, all our ailments will be taken care of. Clearly, we all know of great people of faith who could not have acted more faithfully, and yet they still suffer. So, the whole notion of, "Well, just be a stronger believer and all your problems will be solved," is not the proper conclusion to draw from this story.

But, this woman's example does lead us to embrace the theory that we can do things which can lead to greater healing and wholeness—things that Jesus himself would endorse as means to better health.

This woman wanted to get well, and she was determined to do what she physically could do to get well.

God calls us to take ownership of our bodies and treat them in ways to prevent needless suffering.

The apostle Paul writes in I Corinthians 6, "Glorify God in your body." It's a simple statement but one that is direct in its meaning. Through the preservation and maintenance of the bodies God has given us, we bring God pleasure.

When we watch what we eat, when we stay active through regular exercise, when we take time for Sabbath-keeping to rest and refresh our bodies and minds, we're taking the initiative to reach out to God and we're taking seriously our responsibility to do our part in maintaining our health.

This is an initiative that people of all ages need to embrace, but it's especially important for children and youth today.

We've all heard the discouraging news about childhood obesity. More and more kids are overweight and are getting diagnosed with diabetes at a young age. This is due to a variety of factors, but the central ingredient is that parents, grandparents, teachers, and others in positions of authority aren't teaching the lessons of a healthy lifestyle. Through our words and through our modeling, we've dropped the ball in terms of sharing what it means to glorify God through our bodies.

We can do better, and we must do better to ensure that this generation is not the first to live a shorter lifespan than the generation preceding it.

And so we feel God's touch upon our lives when we take the initiative to reach out to God by choosing responsible and faithful actions.

Touch—whether it be God's loving embrace of us during a crushing time in our life, whether it's a family member or friend reaching out to hold us up in tragedy or celebrate with us in joy, or whether it's each of us taking action to reach out to God so as to be healed like the bleeding woman in Mark 5—in the proper sense can be the most powerful of all of our senses.

Alexander Irvine wrote a novel called *My Lady of the Chimney Corner*. The heroine of the novel goes to a grieving neighbor and, comforting her, puts her hand on her head and says: "God takes a hand whenever he can find it and just does what he likes with it. Sometimes he takes a bishop's hand and lays it on a child's head in benediction. And then he takes the hand of a doctor to relieve the pain, the hand of a mother to guide a child. And sometimes he takes the hand of a poor old creature like me to give comfort to a neighbor. But they're all hands touched by his Spirit, and his Spirit's everywhere lookin' for hands to use."

God's hand comes to us through the hands of others. In what ways will God use our hands to bring healing and wholeness to our lives and to the lives of those we meet?

Entries and Exits
Mark 11:1-11

The Masters, one of golf's greatest tournaments, is just two weeks away. And as it nears, there is some question about whether the game's greatest player over the last two decades will be playing in it. He's one it four times, and a decade ago, experts predicted Tiger Woods would probably win it a half dozen more. He was still young and his victories at Augusta had come with relative ease.

Nobody could stop him. Other players wilted under the pressure of playing against him. His skill in driving, chipping, and putting the ball far exceeded that of his competitors.

But a lot has happened in a decade. Once thought to be unbeatable, much has happened to Tiger Woods so that now, amazingly, he's simply an ordinary pro player. His personal life went south in 2009 as we all know. And his body broke down. And with his injuries went his ability to play at a high level.

Back in January, in his first tournaments since a long injury layoff last year, he shocked the golf world with how badly he played. Every drive missed the fairway, his chip shots sailed over the greens, and his putting was atrocious. (Frankly, as I watched him, I thought, "I have a twin.") I could feel his pain.

Tiger Woods' fall from the pinnacle of golf has been precipitous.

It's a reminder of how quickly one's fortunes can change—whether it be in golf or in any profession or in any personal situation. In our health, in our relationships, change can happen almost in a heartbeat.

Picture yourself in Jerusalem on the day of this grand parade. This scene has been building for weeks and months. This Jesus of Nazareth has been doing things reminiscent of the promised Messiah. He's been healing people in ways that defy explanation. He has been teaching lessons of faith with words meant to emphasize love and justice for all—especially the weak and outcast.

The crowds following him have grown—to the point where they have gathered, at least in this part of Jerusalem, to see him and show in him praise.

The cloaks have been laid down with branches in tow for the grand entry of a king. And the shouts grow louder: "Hosanna! Blessed is the one who comes in the name of the Lord! Hosanna in the highest!"

With good reason, the people whose lives he touched in ways that represent such a positive change from the rulers of the day are giving him his due. This parade is glorious. Much like the parade of children this morning that we saw when they entered the sanctuary, those gathered along the road had to be smiling.

It was a grand entry.

Unlike the crowds that day, however, we have the benefit of hindsight. We know the shouts of praise didn't last. In amazement, we now know the shouts of Hosanna would change to those of "Crucify him" by some. And for others, there would just be silence. No praising, no following, just silent betrayal and then anything but an anointing.

Jesus' fall would, too, be precipitous. As grand as his entry into Jerusalem was, his exit from the world he had taken by storm would be equally defeating and humiliating.

Again, the world can change on a dime. And it certainly did for Jesus throughout that week.

How do we explain this? How do we explain such grand entries and such sad and unexpected exits? In the case of every job firing, or bad diagnosis, or sudden death, or relationship failure, or fall from popularity among friends and admirers, sometimes there can be really no explanation that is good enough.

In Jesus' case, we now believe that his demise was due to a plan that involved his death and the taking on of the suffering and sin of the world. And his exit came about not because of his abandonment of those he loved but by his total embracing of the world with committed care and concern.

Indeed, his leaving of this world did not mean the end of his love—even for those who sentenced him to death or hung with him on the cross. We firmly believe that his exit was a sign of his love—the ultimate sign of anyone's love.

So maybe that's it—maybe that's all we can say when sudden changes occur. When we go from the highest of highs to the lowest of lows and we find no reason for why such changes occur, we do find certitude in the love of Christ—a love that is significant in life but profound in suffering and death.

On our Spring Break trip from a couple weeks ago, we drove south on I-75 for 1000 miles to south Florida. And we drove home 1000 miles on I-75 from south Florida. In both directions, there are many entities that entice motorists to exit the interstate. First of all, there are the rest areas. And I must say that, of all the rest areas we took advantage of in three states, the rest areas in Georgia seemed to be the plushest. I'm not sure that's the primary selling point that the Georgia department of tourism would want to push, but they do rest areas well.

There are, of course, other enticements to exit the interstate. Some of these are not appropriate for good people of faith (these were also found in Georgia). And then there are the blue signs that come in threes: one that lists all the restaurants off the exit, another that lists the places where you can refuel your vehicle, and a third that gives you options for lodging.

And the longer you've been driving, the more enticing these exits become. And you take them, and you eat, refuel, and rest either for short periods of time or overnight.

And then, amazingly and obviously, near the exit is an entrance back on to the interstate. Always. Unless some civil engineer has really fallen down on the job, an entrance back onto the highway is never far away.

Exit and enter. Exit and enter. Entrances provide us the means for getting back on the road. They are always there, soon after the exit.

But unlike signs offering us enticements to exit, there are no signs enticing us to get on the on-ramp. But we don't need enticements for that. Our enticement is built-in. Our enticement is whatever our destination may be—vacation for us on our way down or the comforts of home on our way back.

On these journeys of life that we find ourselves on, there are many exits, many falls. And some of them we don't take willingly. But we have faith that following right behind every fall or exit is always an entry, a chance for redemption, a chance for healing, a chance for new life. That is our enticement to get back on that road, along with the love of God that is with us during every rise and every fall.

Back to Tiger Woods for a minute. Due to several issues, he has seemingly exited his former playing form. And many are saying he will never regain the form he had in his prime. That level of dominance will not be replicated.

But he's only 38 years old. And because we've seen him do what hardly anybody with a golf club in their hands has ever done, none of us—whether we are fans of his or not—should count him out for good. There are still many on-ramps for him on his golfing road.

And we know that the grand entry of Jesus into Jerusalem that we celebrate today was but a prelude to an awful exit from the stage that was to come. And as people of faith who through our sin are partly responsible for that exit, we must take that exit with him this week.

But we also know the rest of the story. That for Jesus, a glorious re-entry would soon come. And we are the beneficiaries of it, because whether we are coming or going, rising or falling, entering or leaving the scene, the love of Jesus Christ undergirds it all.

Thanks be to God.

A Step Ahead
Mark 16:1-8

When I was a kid, we would spend our summer weekends at our cabin at the lake. And we'd usually be up late at night after a full day of swimming, boating, and other things you do at the lake.

This meant that my brother and I were usually not early risers the next morning. Our eyes usually wouldn't open until well after the sun had come up, the first ripples had appeared on the water, and several cars had driven by on the road that went by our place.

As I got older, though, I began to wake with the sunrise more and more. My eyes would open just as it seemed the sun was breaking. And there would be no evidence of anybody stirring in the house.

I'd gently saunter down the steps careful not to make them creak so as to awaken anybody else. I'd go out onto the porch and sit there, convinced that I had beaten everybody else out of bed.

But then I would gaze outside and realize the car was gone. Dad had already been up, gotten dressed, went outside, started the car, and driven away into town for his morning newspaper—all unbeknownst to me. Or the car would be in the driveway, but Dad had already returned from his daily trip and was outside pulling weeds around the house.

He was an early riser, and nobody seemed to be able to beat him out of bed.

It is either delightful or aggravating when somebody is one step ahead of you. If you're a kid and your brother or sister beats you to an opportunity, it can be especially annoying. Or in the case of something you didn't particularly want to participate in, you're more than happy to have a sibling, spouse, or parent get a head start.

In Mark's account of the resurrection, Mary, Mary Magdalene, and Salome (the mother of James and John) went to the tomb very early on the first day of the week with spices to anoint Jesus' dead body. They may have wanted to get there early to get a head start on anybody who may have had intentions to do something else with it. (In those days, the bodies of criminals put to death were simply left for the animals to scavenge, or they were stolen. To have Jesus' body put in a sealed tomb was quite unique.)

They arrived at the burial place to find the stone rolled away and an angel there who says to them, "He isn't here. He's been raised."

This is alarming, of course, to the visitors. They had, even with their close relationship to Jesus, not anticipated this. He wasn't there? He had risen? It didn't make sense.

And then, the angel says something else to the women: "Go, tell his disciples, especially Peter, that he is going ahead of you into Galilee."

Beyond the fright and fear the women had due to the absence of Jesus in the tomb, the reality has also been made clear that Jesus is one step ahead. He was one step ahead of the thieves, he was one step ahead of the two Marys and Salome, and he was one step ahead of the disciples.

He was already on his way back to Galilee, the sight of so much of his ministry, the sight of his many miracles, the sight of more miracles to come.

The story of the resurrection is about many glorious themes: life's triumphant rule over death, God's power over evil, hope that supplants despair. And it's also a reminder of how God is always at least one step ahead of us and the world, not one step behind.

In the creation story in Genesis, God took the first step to create us and everything else out of love and a great need to not be alone.

In the story of the exodus, God through Moses took the first step to deliver the Israelites from bondage, a commitment God made to freedom for all.

In the many accounts of the Old Testament prophets, God, simply because God loved them, took the first steps to restore a sinful people that deserved punishment.

And at Easter, God beats everybody out of the tomb as the ultimate first step toward life—then, now, and in the hereafter.

In the national news during this Holy Week has been this story and the reaction to it about this new Indiana law that evidently was designed to protect religious freedom. I seriously doubt those who wrote the law and voted for it in the Indiana legislature did so to intentionally discriminate against anybody. But the protest against it, whether or not discrimination is at the heart of this law, has revealed one thing this week: There is little or no appetite in this country today for discrimination on the basis of race, gender, or sexual orientation like there once was in our history. Even compared to 10 or 15 years ago, the loud voices that have risen up this week to say "no" to discrimination have perhaps never been heard like this before.

And that is a blessing. And before we arrived at this point in our history, God got here first. We never would have made the strides we have made regarding equality without God first leading the way.

And God is a step ahead of us still, going places that we will thankfully also arrive at eventually. Greater freedom, greater equality, greater peace…we will someday only get to those places because God has taken the first steps to get us there.

We have life because God first chose life over death. We have hope because God first chose hope over despair. We arrive at the tomb tonight and find that he has already left.

All authority and power and dominion to the name that is above all names— Jesus Christ our Lord— now and in the age to come.

"He's Not Here"
Luke 24:1-12

Here now is an entry from the Joey Nieman file. The trials and tribulations of a healthy two-year old are really something to behold. They are exasperating and comedy-inducing all at the same time.

The other night he had one of those moments where nothing seemed to go right for him. Nothing could make him happy. He was upset he couldn't watch the one video he wanted to see. Then he couldn't find the book he wanted to view. Then he was hungry and wanted a snack to eat. Then he really needed some milk to go with his snack.

Between every demand, there was this surge of tears and screams. The correcting of one gross injustice wasn't enough for him. There was always another crisis that the mitigating of the previous one couldn't prevent.

It was an unusual night where both Mom and Dad were simply willing to give in to the demands of their precious child because he was so funny in the ways he unabashedly made his requests known.

Finally, it was time to go to bed. Look out! This is always the Mt. St. Helens of parental torture. You want an eruption that pales in comparison to all other Joey tantrums? Just tell him it's bedtime after he's already had a string of maddening fits. And upon hearing these words from his mother, he looked at her and yelled, "Mommy, you shush it!"

And mommy and daddy just laughed.

Normally a pretty easy-to-please child, there was very little that night that was going to make Joey appreciate the little things in life.

I wish I could tell him that one day he's not going to have those days, that there'll be a moment that's going to come where every day will be framed in the context of what's beautiful and blessed and life-affirming, that there won't be days that are dragged down by crisis and suffering and injustice either in his life or the lives of millions of other human beings.

But it seems that would be too unrealistic.

We are a world that is obsessed with what is wrong. Look at the cover of any major news magazine. The pictures and headlines are ominous.

The cover of this month's *National Geographic* featured a picture of water droplets and the headline: "Water—Our Thirsty World." *Time* magazine's cover this week was titled, "Jobs—Where Are They?" The nightly news and every newspaper are no different, it seems. The stories of suffering and the threats of it are the ones that seem to attract viewers, readers, and listeners.

It seeps into our minds and hearts, and we become trained to fixate on the suffering and whatever else might go wrong.

I was once having a conversation with a woman I knew, and we were contemplating the prospects of her getting a raise at work. "Imagine if you got a $10,000 raise! Wouldn't that be great?" I said.

And I couldn't believe her response. "Yeah," she said, "but I'd just have to pay more income tax then."

Well, yes, but it wouldn't be taxed at 100% no matter the tax bracket. Paying more tax means you're making more money, and that's a good thing. It was that pessimistic mentality, though—something that tells you to look for the worst that could happen instead of the best.

If you're a Presbyterian and you saw the latest trends in membership, this attitude would be just for you. That's because there isn't a lot of good news. In our denomination, membership is shrinking, and the average age of members is rising. More and more churches can't afford full-time ordained clergy, and many are cutting staff and programs.

Bad news reigns and there's increasing reasons to sulk.

According to Luke, what happened on the morning of the first day of the week at the tomb of Jesus was looking to fit in real nicely with this whole theme—mourning, suffering, and pain. The women approached the tomb expecting to find Jesus' body, of course. And they would then weep. Maybe they even would wail. But, they didn't find anything. Two men who appeared to be angels told them a piece of news they weren't expecting: "He's not here."

Wait a minute. That's not the natural progression of events that come with the Good Friday mentality. That's not the next step in the chronicling of a story that was designed to create more wailing and mourning and sadness. To keep with the pattern, Jesus' body should have been there so that the gloom, depression, and travesty of the moment could continue.

But he wasn't there. The women ran back to tell the apostles, but, as so often happens in conversations between men and women, the men incorrectly thought the women were speaking nonsense. Peter had to go see for himself, and upon seeing the strips of cloth lying by themselves in the tomb, he wonders what's happened.

This sets the stage, of course, for Jesus' multiple appearances to the disciples and others—proof that Jesus' absence from that tomb was for real. There was indeed a very good reason to be happy that morning. The women being told that Jesus was not there was the beginning of a reversal of the cycle of lament they had been through.

Now there would be joy, hope, and praise.

You know, so often, we humans—either inside the church or outside—focus so much on suffering and injustice that we don't take time to consider all that is good—to remember that Jesus isn't in the tomb.

We raise money for hurricane and flood victims, we advocate for the curing of terrible diseases, and we raise up the cause of stopping gun violence. We do all this because Jesus called us to, but we do so at the expense of noticing just how beautiful and lovely our world can be. We can't seem to sense the hope in our world. We're stuck with Jesus on the cross and can't get to the tomb to see that he isn't there.

I had to go to a meeting this past week in North Omaha. I took Highway 75 north to 30th street north. And as I went about as far north as I could, guess what I saw? I saw businesses like Hy-Vee and Sonic and Walgreens, I saw schools that were in session, and churches and community centers. I saw kids walking to school and merchants outside their shops doing business.

That's not supposed to be going on there. I thought all that happened there were shootings and stabbings. That's what we see on TV and read in the newspaper. Now, I'm not sure I'd take that same drive at 2 in the morning, but every street at 2 in the morning isn't as safe as it is at 2 in the afternoon.

There's hope there. There's beauty there. Pain and suffering isn't the final word.

Methodist pastor Will Willimon, in a March 2010 article in the *Christian Century*, titled "Now Can We Sing," wrote of two mission trips to Haiti he took with college students in the aftermath of the terrible earthquake there in January. He said, "There was widespread agreement that the most disarming thing about the country was the laughter of the children, along with their raucous singing. How dare they sing when their life expectancy is so horribly short? Was their laughter an escapist respite from the unmitigated tragedy of their lives, or a smart rebuke to our assumption that their lives were trapped in tragedy?

"As darkness fell upon Port-au-Prince after the earth heaved that January night, people danced in the streets and sang hymns. On CNN, Anderson Cooper was incredulous...Those singing-through-their-tears Haitians make me wonder: a truly theological analysis suggests that we may be meant by God for music, destined for joy.

"What if Friday isn't the end of the story? What if God is rewriting human tragedy into surprising comedy? What if Jesus told the truth when he declared, toward the opening of his ministry, that he was turning today's tears into tomorrow's laughter?"

"He's not here," the two men said to the women on Easter morning. Thank God!

Where the Graves Are
John 20:1-18

In an article in *Newsweek* on May 14, 2000, and titled "Play and Pray," author Susan Greenberg described the scene on Easter at American Martyrs Roman Catholic Church in Manhattan Beach, California.

"It was Easter and the Sunday School was hopping. In fact, about 350 preschoolers, many sporting freshly crayoned bunny ears, were bouncing about the Sunday School that Easter Sunday. The "Easter Lady" - a.k.a. Maggie Wright - arrived, dressed in a colorful spring bonnet. 'Merry Christmas!' she bellowed to roars of laughter.

"Actually, I'm here to tell you about Easter, because Easter's kind of confusing," she said.

"The room quieted down as she began to tell a story about an ugly little bulb that blossoms into a beautiful flower. Soon the children are up on their feet, re-enacting the bulb's transformation into shoot, stem and, finally, flower.

"Easter is about how things change," the Easter Lady told them. "What starts to happen in spring? The whole world has died, and it's brought back to life. God brings it all back every year!" Satisfied, the preschoolers dashed off for the Easter egg hunt."

Cute story. Cute way for the Easter Lady to get the message across. The metaphor *seemed* appropriate, because kids enjoy learning things like how plants grow, how they change from one form to another. Plus, they got to act out the story. Maybe they'll have a better memory now of what's important on Easter besides the Easter baskets and egg hunts.

Except for the fact that the metaphor doesn't get it right.

It is so tempting to correlate springtime with resurrection, because we think we see resurrection happening right before our very eyes every year. The grass turns green from an ugly shade of gray. The trees go from bare to budding. There are bright bursts of color when just days before there was no color at all.

"See, resurrection is happening before our eyes. Death has turned into life."

Well, not really. If everything that is now bright and colorful had truly been dead over the wintertime, there would be no color today or any day this spring. A couple weeks ago, I dug up a bush in my front yard that had no color on it when all of the others just like it were again green and growing. It was dead, and it wasn't coming back to life.

What we see happening every spring in the beauty of God's creation around us is not resurrection. It's simply a change of seasons. In winter, plants go dormant—not to die but to hibernate, if you will, until the sunshine returns in its proper form—and the temperatures too.

No, resurrection is different. It's not something that happens in the natural world. There are cycles to the life of a plant. There are cycles to the seasons. There are cycles to the weather and human life.

And although death is a natural part of our own life cycle, true rebirth is not natural. The natural outcome of death is… the end. And there is nothing in our power *we* can do to change that. And there is no natural cycle that brings us back to life, or grants us eternal life.

The good news is what we believe. We do not have the power within us to regenerate. Death brings us to a screeching end. And so we must depend upon the power of God, a true miracle. There is nothing natural about this miracle. On the contrary, it's quite supernatural.

And what's supernatural is an empty tomb on Easter morning.

The German philosopher Friedrich Nietzsche once said, "Only where there are graves is there resurrection."

I'm not sure exactly what Nietzsche meant by that, but it follows what we as people of faith believe. Resurrection can only happen to that which is dead. And we, with the possible of exception of advanced medical technology, cannot bring the dead to life. This power lies only with the risen Christ.

Mary Magdalene was at a grave on the first day of the week when she saw it was empty. And in a frightened conversation with some guy hanging out at that grave, she discovers he's a very much alive Jesus.

If we are willing to go to today's graves, if we are willing to act out in hope of the resurrection by going to those places where there appears to be no life, we stand a better chance of the Lord meeting us.

Jill Duffield, editor of *The Presbyterian Outlook*, writes, "Do not be afraid. For the love of Jesus, keep showing up, even in grief, even in places of pervasive pain. Act out of the hope of resurrection and, lo and behold, all of a sudden the Risen Christ Jesus will meet you, confirming that death doesn't have the last word, life does. In the truth of that promise we keep showing up before dawn, in the middle of the night, and even when everyone else has given up."

We go to those graves expecting and hoping to find a miracle.

In Matthew's translation of the resurrection story, Jesus tells Mary and Mary Magdalene to not be afraid. "Instead," he says, "go and tell my brothers to go to Galilee; there they will see me."

As Michael Curry, presiding bishop of the Episcopal Church, often admonishes his flock: "Go to Galilee." He asks, "Where is your Galilee?

In the streets of the city.

Galilee.

In our rural communities.

Galilee

Galilee in our hospitals.

Galilee in our office places.

Galilee where God's children live and dwell.

In Galilee, you will meet the living Christ for He has already gone ahead of you."

Galilee. Where the graves are. Where there is the resurrected Jesus.

Work and Our Reason for It
Leviticus 19:1-2, 9-18

In the Des Moines Register a few weeks ago, there was a story I found interesting. We've all heard of candy bars that get stuck in vending machines after they've been purchased. This story adds a new dimension to that maddening dilemma.

Robert McKevitt was working the second shift at Polaris Industries' warehouse in Milford, Iowa, when he decided to break for a snack last fall. He says he deposited $1 in a vending machine, selected a Twix bar, and then watched as the candy bar crept forward in its slot, began its descent and was abruptly snagged by a spiral hook that held it suspended in midair.

McKevitt put in another dollar, and still the candy bar didn't budge.

At first, McKevitt's frustration took the customary route: He banged the side of the machine. He tried rocking it back and forth. But when that didn't work, McKevitt walked away…and commandeered an 8,000-pound forklift!

He reportedly drove up to the vending machine, lifted it 2 feet off the concrete warehouse floor — and then dropped it. He allegedly repeated the maneuver at least six times, by which time three candy bars had fallen into the chute for his retrieval.

When a supervisor confronted him, McKevitt allegedly explained he was simply trying to get the snack he had paid for.

He was fired five days later.

In a ruling that became public last month, a state administrative law judge denied his claim for unemployment benefits, saying McKevitt had demonstrated a willful disregard for his employer's interests.

Said McKevitt, "That machine was trouble. They fired me, and now I hear they have all new vending machines there."

McKevitt clearly went a little too far in getting what was rightly his. But I guess we can't help but admire his tenacity.

We can't help but admire the tenacity of all human beings who take initiative to improve their condition. For those who take matters into their own hands—in a lawful and moral way—they are their own deciding factor in their outcomes. It is their hard work, their decision-making, their resolve that leads them to where they are in life. And they wouldn't want it any other way.

In fact, isn't the worst decision any of us could make the decision to not work, not take any action at all? When it comes to parenting or careers or lives of faith, it is far worse to sit idly by rather than risk failure by acting.

When we try, we get results—sometimes not the results we want but some result that's going to tell us where we stand in life. And all of us are looking to find out where we stand.

One year following his second term as President of the United States, Theodore Roosevelt delivered a speech in Paris on April 23, 1910. It was entitled "Citizenship in a Republic." It is a speech worthy of our consideration as citizens but also as people of faith in a very uncertain world. In the speech is a quote that all of us who might be getting a little too content or too lazy should hear.

Said Roosevelt, "It is not the critic who counts; not the one who points out how the strong person stumbles or where the doer of deeds could have done them better. The credit belongs to the one who is actually in the arena, whose face is marred by dust and sweat and blood; who strives valiantly; who errs, who comes up short again and again , because there is not effort without error and shortcoming; but who does actually strive to do the deeds; who knows great enthusiasms, the great devotions, who spends oneself in a worthy cause; who, at the best, knows in the end the triumph of high achievement, and who, at the worst, if failing at least fails while daring greatly, so that one's place shall never be with those cold and timid souls who neither know victory nor defeat."

I had no idea until recently that Roosevelt had served as police commissioner of New York City prior to his time in the White House. And his term as commissioner was characterized with reforms and modernization, very often in the face of entrenched opposition from traditionally corrupt players.

Roosevelt didn't sit idly by, because worse than making the wrong move, in his judgment, was making no move at all.

I'm not sure what God is calling us to do, but I'm confident that God is not calling us to sit idly by. And our aim should not just be to improve our own lives, which is very noble. It should primarily be out of a response to the God who made us.

In the text from Leviticus, God knows that Moses has a bunch of followers who are active people. They are doers, like we should all strive to be. But in God's instructions, there is a command to act properly—not so that they could merely protect themselves and others, but because they were acting in response to the God who made them.

Throughout the text, there is a constant refrain that God doesn't let them forget: I am the Lord your God. God repeats it over and over—just in case they lose sight of the fact that the God who calls them and us to action should never be forgotten.

Our actions should always be done in the context of a God who made us, who is always with us, and always concerned that those actions are giving God glory and praise.

As empowered as we are and should be in our lives to take action, we always stand in deference to this God who desires that we put concern for God and for others on equal if not greater footing than concern for ourselves.

We stand in the shadow of God, not in our own shadow. And so, our actions should reflect that allegiance to the God who made us: whether it be in how we retrieve a stuck candy bar from the vending machine, how we parent our children, or how we look out for the poor. The words, "I am the Lord your God" should always be in our ears and in our minds, calling us to act in ways that are truly reflective of blessed and appreciative children of God.

No More Beans!
Luke 24:13-35

What keeps you from recognizing someone who was once so recognizable? As time goes by and the longer we've gone in seeing someone we once recognized so easily, the more difficult it is to not recognize that person when they come back into our presence.

Maybe it's weight gain or weight loss, maybe it's the effects of aging, maybe it's a change in hair color or hair loss, maybe it's the glasses they now wear or the clothing style they now embrace. Whatever the reason, there are moments when it takes some work on our part to recognize someone we once knew.

A few months ago, my family and I were in downtown Knoxville. And we were sitting outside having ice cream at a place on Gay Street on a beautiful afternoon. And we noticed there was a whole bunch of commotion going on across the street. It looked like they were filming a scene for a TV show or a movie, because there were cameras and other equipment and a bunch of people milling around.

And then there were the quiet murmurings we heard: "Do you see him? Look, over there, over there. It's Burt Reynolds!"

And so, we looked. And an older gentleman was sitting on a director's chair with a few people standing around him. He wasn't moving well; in fact, he was just sort of sitting there looking rather disinterested.

"That's Burt Reynolds?" I wondered. (My kids asked, "Who's Burt Reynolds?")

As it turned out, it was Burt Reynolds—in town filming a movie. And all I could think was, "Wow, that Smokey and the Bandit movie from 1977 was a long time ago."

It didn't look like the Burt Reynolds I remembered. The passing of time can take a toll on all of us.

For some reason, late in the day of Jesus' resurrection, two disciples were travelling to the small village of Emmaus. And they had heard what had happened to Jesus—his sentencing to death, his crucifixion on the cross, and then the rumor that some of the women had gone to Jesus' tomb to find his body missing and angels telling them he was alive again.

They were discussing all these things while walking down this road when the resurrected Jesus arrived on the scene and began walking with them. And for some reason, they didn't recognize him.

And that's hard to believe. After all, it had been just a matter of hours since they had seen Jesus. Decades, years, or even months had not gone by since their last encounter. It was just a couple of days since they had seen him. And because they were his disciples, they would have known intimately what he looked like.

Regardless, they assume on this day he's somebody else. When they reached Emmaus, the disciples urged this man to stay with them. And he did. And it wasn't until they sat down at the dinner table and Jesus broke bread in front of them that they recognized who he was.

It was that familiar gesture—that breaking of the bread, maybe at his Last Supper with all the disciples—that opened their eyes to his identity.

There are so many triggers that lead our minds to identify with a person or event.

I've always heard that one of the best things any church could do (if it were possible) would be to bake loaves of bread in the church kitchen every communion Sunday so that the aroma of freshly baked bread would flow through the sanctuary and trigger the memories of a special meal with family. Indeed, the Lord's Supper is a coming together with family to enjoy a meal that Christ has prepared.

There are other sounds, smells, and pictures that trigger memories or an awareness of an event taking place.

The smell of coffee brewing or bacon cooking on the stove would awaken me from sleep when I was a kid and tell me that morning had arrived.

Indeed, food can have this effect.

One of the outreach projects our former church in Nebraska supports is a prison ministry called Crossroads Connection. Each Sunday evening, inmates from the Omaha Work Release Center are picked up by sponsors of the program and driven to Underwood Hills Presbyterian Church not far from there. And once they arrive, other churches in the presbytery take turns each week leading a worship service and serving dinner to the inmates and their families.

The Bellevue church does this about 4-5 times a year and we always wanted the meal to be a good meal. We also tried to make it a simple meal.

The first few times we brought the meal, we served barbeque. And one of the side dishes that goes great with barbeque is baked beans. After the meal, we noticed that not many of the baked beans were getting eaten. These baked beans were pretty tasty, but the roaster was still quite full after everybody had eaten.

We came to find out that baked beans were a staple back at the center where the inmates lived. They got beans in some form all the time. And when these folks arrived at our meal, one look at our baked beans triggered thoughts of a home they didn't want to be reminded of. They were saying to us, "No more beans."

From that point on, we scrapped the baked beans during our visits to Crossroads. Instead, our side dishes were always homemade salads. Those salads would disappear in no time, because they're tasty but also because they triggered memories of home and the hospitality they remembered receiving at home from their mothers or grandmothers or spouses.

"No more beans." Instead, the message to us was "more pasta salad, potato salad, green salad, Jello salad, and all those things mom used to make."

And in a strange way, maybe those inmates sensed in that church fellowship hall the presence of Christ in that moment—comfort, hope, and love.

When the two disciples recognized Jesus in their midst through the breaking of the bread, their response is worthy of mention.

What would have happened to the good news if those disciples had said to themselves after Jesus appeared to them, "Wow. That was awesome! Let's keep this a secret. We got to see something the others haven't."

But that's not what they did. They went to Jerusalem and told the other disciples, "The Lord really has risen!"

When we've seen something extraordinary—something we can only attribute to the presence of the risen Christ—we can't help but share it.

As the theologian Karl Barth said, "Anybody who simply stops on the sidewalk, looks upward, and points soon draws a crowd of onlookers, each one attempting to see what captures the gaze of another. The witness is interesting because the witness points to some great truth that's more interesting than the witness."

Christ resurrected is surely much more interesting than the rest of us speaking about it. And yet, the more we speak of it—words and actions—the more others will stop and look up and see what we've seen.

And so, we clamor for "no more beans!" Instead, we beg for those signs that speak of love, hope, and comfort. We beckon God to reveal Godself yet again—in the middle of churchy words and music during Sunday morning worship, in the presence of a friend who comes alongside us during a time of pain and suffering, in the beautiful hues of a rainbow overlooking the grave of a loved one we have just buried, in the celebratory spirit fanned at a gathering of friends marking a successful accomplishment, or in the quiet stillness of a back porch at nightfall.

We invite God to enter our space and make known the resurrected Christ.

In the words of the familiar Clara Scott hymn, "Open my eyes that I may see glimpses of truth Thou hast for me; place in my hands the wonderful key that shall unclasp and set me free. Silently now I wait for Thee, ready my God Thy will to see; open my eyes, illumine me, Spirit divine."

On the Road to Resurrection
Romans 6:1b-11

We are always on a journey. Our lives are about taking journeys to places here and there. And because we are on so many journeys, we have slogans that describe those journeys: In college baseball, if you want to make it to the College World Series next month, you must travel the Road to Omaha. In college basketball, it's the Road to the Final Four. In the movies, we've heard of great films like "The Road to El Dorado" and the "Road to Perdition." If we're lost, we often say we're traveling on the "road to nowhere." Or if we're getting well after a long illness, we like to say we're on the road to recovery.

Whether we are physically traveling to a new destination or mentally looking for a way to describe where our hearts or minds are at a particular moment, we are always moving—always journeying to a different place.

The same is true of us spiritually. We can be on the road to despair at times, which I'm sure all of us have travelled more than once. That road is filled with all kinds of misfortune. The loss of a family member or a job often finds us on this road. The loss of everything we own in a tornado or a 500-year flood might lead us down this path, too.

The flooding here from a few summers ago left many in our community travelling this road, some more severely than others.

When things like this happen, it seems we find only darkness on our path, with no hope on the horizon.

Our sinfulness can also lead us down this same desperate road. We get wrapped up in the activities that go against what God would want us to do, to the point where we again see no way out—no hope at the end of the road. And it's our rebelliousness and stubbornness that often take us there.

Once upon a time, a man was driving on a winding road, when he saw a "Road Closed" sign up ahead. Not seeing any construction taking place, he ignored the sign and drove on. He discovered the construction around the next bend and had to turn around and go back to follow the detour.

As he approached the blockade, he saw on the back of the "Road Closed" sign, in hand-scrawled letters, a message: "Told you so!"

We do things like this all the time, ignoring the warning signs placed in front of us to get where we think our selfish intentions should take us.

For people of faith in Jesus Christ, we have been placed on a different road, a road not leading to despair and death but a road leading to newness of life. We haven't placed ourselves on that road; instead, we have been turned around and pointed in a different direction by someone else. The road in front of us now doesn't lead to darkness, but to light. It leads not to confusion and hopelessness but to hope and new life.

This road is the road to resurrection. And we have been placed on that road by Jesus himself.

In Romans 6, the apostle Paul reminds us that we have been buried with Christ by baptism into death, so that, just as Christ was raised from the dead by the glory of God, so we too might walk in newness of life.

Our old selves were crucified with Jesus on that cross so that the body of our sin might be destroyed, and we might no longer be enslaved to sin.

Christ has placed us on the road to resurrection by going with us deep down into the waters of baptism and cleansing us of the dirtiness that comes with our sin. And so now instead of only going down deep into those same dark waters, we are now coming back out of them with Christ. Like the ever-brightening water at the top of a swimming pool, we see the light ahead and anticipate the new life that awaits us when we come to the surface of the water.

That is the road to hope, the road to new life, the road to resurrection.

I once counseled a young woman who found herself on the road to despair. She was married, but her relationship to her husband had become rocky. Alcohol had become a dominant part of both of their lives; infidelity was present as well. And the behavior of husband and wife was taking a toll on the lives of their children.

She came to me feeling as though she was on the road to despair, the road to nowhere. She had tried to repair her marriage before and it hadn't worked. She had tried to stop drinking before and it hadn't worked. She believed there was no hope. Still, something inside of her made her reach out and ask for help. She didn't know it at the time, but already she had been turned around and placed on the road to the resurrection.

The word she received from me was that there was hope for her. And even though the days ahead would still be difficult (some of them even more difficult), God loved her and was pointing her down a road to a better place—greater self-care and greater prosperity for her kids. Her old self had already been crucified with Christ; no longer would she be enslaved to sin.

Being on the road to resurrection doesn't necessarily mean we've fully arrived at our destination. After all, we will always have the tendency to sin. It would be impossible for us not to do so.

Clearly, the full glory of resurrection life is not a present reality — it still lies off in the distance, like a beautiful oasis on the horizon. We're on the road to resurrection, for sure, but we haven't quite reached the point where we can put the car in park and relax, knowing we've finally arrived.

The good news for us today is we're moving in the right direction. In fact, we've already crossed the border and have left the world of death and sin behind us.

In Christ, we now have the potential not to sin. And that is good news.

Our task today is to remind ourselves of which road we are on. In Paul's telling the Romans of this good news—this newness of life in which they are walking—he needs the Romans to believe something has happened to them, once and for all. If they will see themselves as dead to sin and wrongdoing, as corpses beyond the influence of either, they will look elsewhere for the source of their life and liveliness. He must startle or shock the Romans into seeing themselves—and so into living—as they never have before.

We too must work at the images we have of ourselves. Because of what Christ has done, we are not destined for the road of sin and death, but are instead already placed on the road to resurrection and newness of life.

This is graduation season, the end of one journey for graduates and soon the beginning of another. On the road to graduation have been potholes, storms, detours, scenic views, and great anticipation. Our high school graduates' parents can vouch for that.

And soon they will enter down different roads—college for the three graduates we recognize today. And yet, we can remind them that as they travel down this new road, they are also travelling a parallel road. It is a road of resurrection gifted to us by Jesus. And no matter the twists and turns they take on their new paths, light resides at the end of their spiritual path. No matter what happens to them on their other journeys, they will be just fine on the road to resurrection.

In the midst of our joys and disappointments, how will we live? Amid unexpected turns and twists on our journeys that often bring great change, what will sustain us? A path to resurrection, cleared by Christ himself, is the right road.

Passing the Baton
Luke 24:44-53

On Wednesday of this week, my mother had some more surgery on the aneurism in her brain that was discovered last year. And it all went very well. She went home the next day.

My dad and I spent the afternoon on Wednesday in the surgery waiting room in the Clarkson Tower at Nebraska Medical Center. That's where all family members are sent after they say farewell to their loved ones as they are wheeled into surgery.

And for those of you who've waited for family members like this, you know the drill. You sit and sit and sit. Hopefully, you've brought along something to do to pass the time.

As you sit there for hour after hour, your lifeline to what's going on behind the walls of the waiting area is the waiting room attendant. This is the person who relays information to you from the operating room as to whether the doctors are just beginning the operation, are halfway through, or have just moved your loved one into recovery.

And at Clarkson, there's a woman who fills this role with great grace and charm. I don't know her name, but I've seen her there many times when I've been with my family and families of members of the church who are having surgery.

If you're there to wait, the first thing is to go in and introduce yourself to this nice woman so that she knows who you're following. She has a list of patients, and she finds the name of the one you're with. She then writes down your name and phone number, so she knows who to communicate with when news comes to her.

So, I introduced myself to her on Wednesday and she exclaimed, "Oh, Matt, sure it's good to see you." It was as if she'd been waiting for me and remembered me from the last time I was there. "I tell you what," she said, "Go ahead and get settled here. I see it's about lunchtime, and they're just getting started with your Mom. Now would be a good time to go and grab some lunch; and when you get back, check in and maybe we'll have an update on how far along the docs are."

"Oh, yes, yes," I thought. "That's what we should do. We should get settled and then go to lunch. It makes perfect sense."

And so, we went and ate, relaxing while knowing we were doing what we should be doing. And then we returned to the waiting area to find the smile of the attendant again.

"How was lunch? Great, Matt. Well, make yourself comfortable here and when we hear something, we'll let you know."

And I felt so much better because someone had guided us in what we should do and had comforted us by making us feel cared for and at home.

In that setting, we (my dad and I) were passed from the caring hands of the pre-op nurse who told us where to go and what to do when we arrived that morning to this waiting room attendant who would make sure we endured the wait with peace.

Then, when the surgery was over, and Mom had left recovery, she went to the ICU, where we also would be passed along to the nursing staff in that unit.

On that day, nobody did all the work. When we met with my mom's surgeon after the procedure, he gave us great joy and comfort when he told us all was well and showed us on his iPhone the picture he had taken of how good the aneurism looked. Then he said goodbye.

We wished he could have walked with her up to ICU and stayed with her there as she recovered. But, no, that's not how it works. He passed Mom along to nurses and doctors upstairs who would guide her on the next leg of her journey before she went home.

The baton of care is passed so often in a hospital setting, whether it's the patient or the family who is being taken care of. Nobody does it by him or herself, even when you think you'd want one person doing it all.

This is true of many avenues of life—nobody does it all.

It's the end of the school year, and last Sunday night, our youngest son, Joey, cried when I told him that this past week would be the last week he would have Mrs. Wendling for a teacher downstairs at Welcome School. He just didn't understand why she couldn't be his teacher next year and the next year and the next year.

For students' education, the baton is passed from teacher to teacher to teacher.

Not always is the one who starts a job the one who finishes the job.

Why is it that, after Jesus' resurrection from the grave, he spends time with his disciples again? Why not just immediately ascend into heaven? It would have saved him the awkwardness of having to leave the disciples a second time.

Here at the end of Luke 24, he's teaching them one final time. He opens their minds to understand the scriptures and then, after leading them out as far as Bethany, he lifts his hands, blesses them, and is carried up into heaven.

He would continue to guide them and teach them, but not in ways that the disciples probably hoped for or counted on. In an instant, he was gone. Jesus had earlier promised them that the Holy Spirit would be sent as their advocate, their helper. But at the moment, the disciples probably didn't get how the work of Jesus would continue without his physical presence.

Christ knew, however, that the baton had to be passed. The word would go from his physical being to the Spirit, and the Spirit would come to person after person, prophet after prophet, leader after leader, spreading the Word over hundreds and thousands of years all over the world.

In the great tradition of Moses, who labored as the God's chief messenger for years and years but who was forbidden from finally entering the promised land with the Israelites and who passed the torch to Joshua for the final leg of the journey, Jesus knew it would take others carrying the Word in the absence of his physical presence in order to complete the job.

Rarely does one person lead us from the start of our journey to its conclusion. And it is so true of our faith. The Sunday School teacher we have as a preschooler is different from the one we have in 2nd or 3rd grade, who's different from the youth leader we have in high school, who's different from the one who guides us as a college student. Our life journeys as adults take us from place to place, where we meet and become close to pastors or other Bible teachers for short periods of time.

And the departures from those who've mentored us and taught us are sad; but at the end of our life journeys, we're able to look back and see how blessed we were to have been molded by so many different voices, so many different personalities, so many different styles.

The fullness of the word, Jesus seems to say with his ascension into heaven, only becomes apparent when it is shared through the personalities and passions of a variety of God's children. Christ wanted all his children to hear the word and follow him through the colorful tapestry of messengers he would place before them.

We should be thankful that the baton that is God's word is not controlled by one messenger. It is framed, articulated, and crafted by person after person before being passed on to the next. And the richness of God's people is what causes God's word to remain fresh, challenging, instructive, and full of hope.

There is always a great sadness when someone we love dies. We miss different qualities of different people. And if we're really attached, we miss their legacy of wisdom and mentoring. When that special someone dies, a void is left; and that void will be filled. It will be filled by that new mentor, that new teacher, that new doctor, that new boss, that new friend.

And though we mourn, we grow. And maybe we grow into that part ourselves. Maybe we more quickly become that mentor, teacher, or guide to somebody else. And maybe the world will be enhanced in ways it could not have before.

Jesus ascended into heaven. And yet, 2000 years after he did so, the Word is present—stronger than ever. Through the leadership and investment of so many, God's word is being proclaimed in word and deed. Thanks be to God for those who've taken the baton and those who will have it passed to them in years to come.

May I See Some ID, Please?
Romans 5:1-5

I want to tell you a story this morning about a man named Terry. You just might know him. Terry is a husband and father of two teenage girls. He and his family live in a middle-class suburb in a metropolitan area such as ours.

Terry was raised in a stable home, although his father died when he was very young. His mom remarried, and his stepfather became the father he never really knew. As a young boy, Terry developed a love for gadgets, tinkering with everything from remote-controlled cars to the primitive video games that existed during his childhood. He moved from interest to interest, hardly stopping to sit and rest.

Terry's interests in so many things led him to a busy and successful life as an adolescent and teenager. He was a good student—especially in math and science courses that really pushed his analytical skills. Other kids looked to him for guidance and help in getting through review sessions or studying for quizzes.

Terry worked hard, but he played hard as well. He loved baseball. In the summertime, when not working at the local grocery store as a teen, he was hitting doubles and triples for his high school team and manning third base on the infield. His team nearly reached the state tournament two out of his four years.

His active and achieving lifestyle expressed itself in college, too. He earned scholarships to the local university, where he earned his degree in computer science and graduated magna cum laude. He was always on the go. His roommate in college hardly ever saw him—there were always so many exams to study for, projects to complete, students to lead, social gatherings to go to, and money to be earned in part-time jobs.

As an adult, marriage and fatherhood helped him maintain his on-the-go lifestyle. His work as a software developer was more than full-time and paid the bills, but he found himself more consumed with coaching his daughter's softball teams, his leadership on his homeowners' association board, his work with a local Habitat for Humanity chapter, and his desire to tinker in his garage.

At the height of an obscenely hectic stretch one month, he got to thinking about his identity. He was extremely busy with stuff to do and had little free time. And yet, he questioned who he was. "That's silly," he told himself. "You're a devoted husband to Jean and father to the girls. You're a family man. And you're an accomplished developer. Your work has been singled out by company brass numerous times for its excellent design and effectiveness. And you're a servant of the community with all your volunteer work. Of course, you know who you are. You've achieved and will go on to achieve so much."

But Terry still couldn't shake the feeling—the feeling that he still couldn't with absolute certainty put his finger on who he was.

Maybe you recognize Terry. All of us probably have a little Terry inside of us. From a young age, we are told our lives are what we make of them. And that we can become anything we want to become. And so, we set out on our quest to be the best possible teacher, or doctor, or contractor or sales person, or entrepreneur, or mother we could be. And to do this, we sign up to hone the skills we'll need to succeed in these areas. We go to school, we get involved in organizations, we read and model ourselves after others. And we get feedback along the way as to how we're doing.

Speaking of feedback, at the beginning of my sophomore year in high school, I remember my veteran Algebra II teacher telling my parents he hadn't seen anybody in his Algebra classes as gifted as me since Teresa Rice, who was four years older than me. (She had gone on to become an actuary with a big life insurance company and was making a lot of money.) Well, this made my parents feel excited about their kid's potential.

It wasn't long after I got my first quarter grades for Algebra II that it became apparent it was time for my teacher to start thinking about retirement. That's because my grades didn't come close to his lofty assessment of my abilities in math. That class would be my last math course in high school. And now I'm the farthest thing from an actuary I could ever be.

Feedback can be deceiving; but it does help us make choices of who we will become.

We mostly look for our identities in what we *do*. And it's what we do that seems to give us our place in the world. How many times, when getting acquainted to somebody we haven't met before, have we been introduced by our profession? "This is Matt; he's the pastor at First Presbyterian Church." Or, "Let me introduce Willis; he's an architect." Or, "This is Julie, she's a teacher." It's the identity we've constructed for ourselves.

The first few words of the book of Genesis in the Old Testament are "In the beginning, God created…" And the Bible ends in Revelation with another future that is also created by God.

Pastor Craig Barnes, in his book *The Pastor as Minor Poet*, writes, "This means that all things, even the dust with which humanity was created, derive their existence from God. So when we seek a different identity derived from anything other than God, we don't actually become different but only return to the nothingness we were before God created our lives."

All of us falsely believe we can reach for something other than what we have been given by the Creator, and that those things or titles we reach for will give us a place in the world that will make crystal clear who we are and leave us satisfied.

Instead, our Christian faith tells us we cannot really create our own identity. It's been created for us already by God. And that identity is one, according to Paul, where we have already been justified by faith. We don't need to do anything to find our place. God has given us a place already as redeemed and forgiven through Jesus Christ. It's not about what we do; it's about who we are, whose we are, and who we have been since the beginning.

Since we moved here to Bellevue, I've been so impressed by all the great people I've met with military ties. They—you—are proud of their service to their country and feel fortunate to have made careers (many of you) in military service.

But in my time here, I've never met a veteran or someone on active duty who has ever put their rank or their job ahead of their identity as a child of God made right by their faith in Jesus Christ. In fact, while many of you are highly decorated veterans, I don't know much about your careers. And that's because in the settings in which we interact, it's not as important to you as the identity that has been created for you by God.

Indeed, the fallen heroes whom we honor on Memorial Day tomorrow are those who first and foremost claim their identity as servants—even though they were terrific soldiers, sailors, airmen, or Marines. What was important to them was who they were, not what they did.

Our church here is fortunate to have a bell outside in the bell tower that is rung every Sunday morning before worship. Why do we ring that bell? Part of the reason is that it's a carryover of a tradition that was started at our old church building downtown. Ringing the bell has historically been a method of calling people to the church for worship. You heard the bell and you then knew it was time for church.

But maybe there is another reason for ringing that bell. Maybe we ring it not only to summon people for worship, but also because we want to tell our community that we have something to say, something important to say, something our culture perhaps would never say. And what we have to say is this: We are justified or made right with God not because of anything we have done, not by any identity we have constructed for ourselves. Our identity has been given to us already: we are forgiven and restored children of God through the saving grace of Jesus Christ. Therefore, we can have peace.

Of course, deciding what one's gifts and talents are, working to maximize those talents, and achieving great independence and success through those gifts are good things. Our world needs more of that independent and achieving spirit. But in the end, those achievements can never supplant what God has already done for us in Christ.

If someone, besides a patrolman on the highway, were to stop and ask me to show them some identification, I wish I could have something to show them or tell them that would say, "In life and in death, I belong to God." Husband to Jenni, father to Jacob and Joey, pastor, citizen—all important pieces of who I am. But nothing exceeds God's claim on my life.

That's a story for us to tell to the nations.

God Shed His Grace on Thee
Genesis 22:1-14

Today we come to one of the most difficult stories to accept in all of scripture. It's so difficult that many preachers tend to not preach on it when it comes around on this Sunday in the Revised Common Lectionary. When I considered whether to include it as a focus today, I decided, because you're here on a summer Sunday when not a lot of other people are, you can handle this text from Genesis 22.

It's a story that makes us cringe more than a little bit. It's a story that makes us wonder why God would choose to take the action God does: The call of Abraham to sacrifice his son, Isaac, only to call it off at the last possible moment.

This is a story about being radically obedient to God, even when we couldn't imagine carrying out a task Abraham was asked to complete.

We learn through this story that God is both ridiculously demanding and a ridiculously generous provider.

Now, let's take this story and set it aside for a few moments. We'll come back to it.

This is Independence Day weekend, a great time to appreciate the blessing of being Americans.

My dad served in the army and instilled in me a love of country from an early age. I was taught explicitly as a kid how to act whenever the flag was raised during the playing of the National Anthem: with reverence and honor for what the flag stands for. There was to be no messing around when that flag was presented, and that anthem was played. Too many people died for what that flag stands for.

The last congregation I served in Nebraska was a stone's throw from Offutt Air Force Base and Strategic Command. That church was full of military veterans who served this country heroically. Of all the funerals I did for members of that church, I'd say at least a third were conducted with full military honors—the folding of the flag, the three-gun salute, and the playing of taps by an honor guard.

There was the funeral for Buck Eidenmiller who landed on Omaha Beach in 1941. He fought courageously and ended up supporting the effort as a mess hall cook. In fact, he cooked so well, officers from other units would often search his mess hall out. When he returned home from the war, his family often asked him why he didn't cook at home. He said, "I only cook for hundreds at a time."

There was also the funeral for a young man named Chuck Radosta, a Navy pilot who we buried at the National Cemetery in Minneapolis, Minnesota, on a very cold January afternoon. He left behind a young wife and two young girls who to this day miss him terribly but give thanks for his life as an American patriot.

When you're around people like this, you can't help but be in awe for what this nation stands for—a country so great that so many risked and sacrificed their lives for it.

Last week, we went sightseeing in Washington, D.C. While Jacob had been there before on a school trip, the rest of us had never been there. It was fabulous in many ways: We saw the National Symphony Orchestra at the Kennedy Center, we saw the Nationals play the Cubs at Nationals Park, we went to some of the many, many incredible museums that are there. But by far, the best part of the trip for me was our visits to Arlington National Cemetery and the many memorials.

While we're certainly not a perfect country with progress left to make, we're a very good and noble people who have been called to reach greater heights of freedom and justice. The Lincoln Memorial reminds you of this, the Martin Luther King, Jr. Memorial reminds you of this. And then you walk to the memorials that honor those who fought for the freedoms we enjoy—like the Vietnam Memorial and the World War II Memorial—and you are overcome with gratitude for these people who fought and died to ensure the freedoms we enjoy.

With all the rancor and division, we have in our country today, a visit to the nation's capital enhances and bolsters your confidence in how great America still is. My patriotism is soaring after last week.

On this Independence Day weekend, it's good to give thanks to God for all that's good about America.

I know you all join me in giving thanks for this country. We regularly give thanks during worship for the blessings we enjoy as a free people in America.

We love our country. Many of you have served in the military as a response to that love and some of your children and grandchildren have served. We recognize our veterans every year, and we sing patriotic songs in worship occasionally (we're closing today by singing the Navy hymn).

And yet, when we gather in this space on Sunday mornings and other occasions, we do so not to *worship* America (as much as we *love* America) but to worship God. We worship the God of Abraham who, we discovered today, demands so much of us (like he strangely demanded the near-sacrifice of Isaac by Abraham) and who gives so much to us (God's sacrifice of his only Son, Jesus, for all humanity is the ultimate proof).

It is God who has intervened in the world and helped create this nation we all love and every other nation that promotes peace, freedom, and justice for all. It is God who shed his grace on us—in abundance. When we walk into this worship space, there should be no doubt as to who we worship. It is the triune God—Father, Son, and Holy Spirit.

As Americans, we should always give thanks for the freedoms we enjoy—even the freedom to behave in ways we adamantly disagree with.

But when we worship on Sundays in this space, we only worship one entity—the God who calls us to extreme obedience and the God who loves us outlandishly.

All of us are united as proud Americans; but more importantly, all of us are united as beloved children of God.

To Whom We Belong
Ephesians 1:3-14

I guess this is the Word of the Lord. I say, "I guess," because this passage from Ephesians is a difficult one to unpack.

I was trying hard to do so this week and had a difficult time landing on any specific part of it that captured my interest. In reading it and re-reading it, however, I did become intrigued by Paul's use of the Greek word υἱοθεσία (*we-oh-thee-see-a*) in verse 5. The New Revised Standard Version of the Bible translates the word as "adoption."

"[God] destined us for *adoption* as his children through Jesus Christ," Paul says.

God brought us in and claimed us as God's own. Through God's great generosity, we belong to God.

This past week, our family had a bit of a stay-cation with some of our very good friends from Nebraska, Ryan and Mandi and their two girls.

It felt like we did it all. We went to Dollywood on Monday, we hiked to Abrams Falls in Cades Cove on Wednesday, and we went tubing on the Little River in Townsend on Thursday—among other things.

When I was standing in line with Joey to ride the Firechaser roller coaster at Dollywood, it occurred to me that when we got on to that rollercoaster we belonged to it. There was no backing out of it once it took off. Everybody else who voluntarily locked themselves into the seats of those cars became equal. It didn't matter one's income level, gender, sexuality, education level, or where one lived. We were all the same for those few moments—we were captives of the Firechaser.

We were captives of the mountains during our hike on Wednesday, too. We belonged to the river as we floated down it in Townsend on Thursday. All of us strangers together—equal and bowing to the twists and turns of the river for two hours.

This is what happens when you are adopted—either temporarily or permanently. You belong to that which or to whom is doing the adopting.

We have parents in this congregation who have adopted their kids, and I have so enjoyed hearing your adoption stories. Your children are fortunate to have come under the wings of such loving parents, and you are so fortunate to have been blessed by your children's presence in your lives.

Moved by a strong calling to love and nurture a child, you reached out with your own God-given gifts and embraced a child in need—rescuing, consoling, and nurturing boys and girls who otherwise may not have experienced those gifts. They belong to you and you belong to them.

Adoption comes in other forms, too, of course. Anybody who goes down to the Humane Society and comes home with a dog or a cat is an adoptive parent—rescuing an animal from a life that otherwise may not last too much longer or be too pleasant.

The apostle Paul, in using a term like adoption, clearly recognized that each of us at one point is in a state of being orphaned. We have been left behind and neglected with nobody to take us under their wings. But what's different about us compared to a child living in an orphanage or a cat living at the pound is that, in a spiritual sense, we have typically done something to leave us orphaned. Unlike children or pets left alone through no fault of their own, our sin and rebellion is often what leaves us looking for a rescuer, somebody to take us in and call us their own.

Paul tells us in Ephesians that we have been adopted; we have been taken in by God. We have been forgiven and cleansed of what ails us even though our isolation and abandonment may have been our own faults.

Through the grace of Jesus Christ, despite what we have or have not done, we have not been left alone with nobody to claim us. God has adopted us through the blood of Jesus Christ—redeemed us by his grace.

Jesus himself said that we would not be left alone. In the 14th chapter of John, he says to his disciples on the occasion of his last supper with them, "I will not leave you as orphans." Those disciples included, of course, Peter, the one who would deny him shortly thereafter.

Even the disciples, Jesus' most trusted and devoted followers, were not immune from the sinfulness that would have otherwise left them alone without God's providence and care. Because of his loving sacrifice, however, they would feel God's loving embrace. They belonged to God and forever with God they would be.

You and I, in life and in death, belong to God. Despite all we do to displease God, God has adopted us as God's sons and daughters. Despite the hardship we've endured or the painful actions we have taken to hurt God and others, we have a place in this world and in the life to come.

And this is true, we must recall, of all God's children. Outside of the friendly confines of our congregation, in the diversity of other Christian churches, and in the diversity of people of other religions or no religion at all, everyone belongs to God. Everyone is beloved.

When it seems all others have left us or aren't showing the love we crave, know that the first and best lover remains: the God who has adopted us as sons and daughters. Like that river we can't get out of when we are tubing down it or like that rollercoaster that we can't get out of when we are riding its rails, we can't escape the love of the greatest lover.

I suspect that sometimes—maybe even many times—you come to church on Sundays looking for something to help you live a better life. You look for assistance to guide you through challenges or to help you succeed.

I don't have much in that regard for you today. Instead, I have something better: I have a simple reminder that we are beloved—all of us. We are adopted—through Jesus Christ. And it's not temporary custody like that of a rollercoaster or a rolling river. It is permanent.

Due to a loving parent who will not leave us abandoned, we have a place in the family of God.

In a world in which it seems there is little good news, that is good news today. We celebrate it by praising the One who has not forgotten us.

What Matters
Matthew 15:10-20

Back in June, I served as a commissioner to this year's General Assembly of the Presbyterian Church USA in Detroit.

As you've heard, it was an important gathering of our highest governing body, with decisions made that thrilled some in the church and disappointed others.

Without a doubt, when we all left Detroit after a long week, we were tired and ready to go home. My flight was not due to leave Detroit until late in the afternoon of the final day of the event, a Saturday. I was due to preach and baptize three children at the Bellevue church the next morning. As you might expect, I was anxious about my flights.

My flight from Detroit to Chicago never took off due to bad weather in Chicago. The United gate agent rebooked me on a Delta flight for later that evening, direct to Omaha. So, I had to take a shuttle to the Delta terminal, go through security a second time, and then take a train to my gate.

I was nervous. I got to the gate in plenty of time, however, and we boarded the plane quickly with time to spare.

Just before the door was closed, a young family bounded onto the plane. First, there was the young dad, somewhat out of breath and flush in the face. He was leading his young daughter, probably 3 or 4 years old, who wondered where she should go.

"All the way to the back," he said.

Next came the young mother. She too was flush in the face and somewhat tired. Clearly, she was stressed out. Most likely, they had all been running to catch this flight. She was also weighed down by bags she was carrying and the anxiety of not knowing if they would get there on time.

In front of her was their young son, probably 7 or 8. As the two of them came on board, she was visibly upset by all that was going on, to the point of tears. And upon seeing the tears of his mother, this young boy, acting like a very mature young man, stopped in the middle of the aisle, with all the other passengers watching him, went back to his mother, patted her arm, and said, "It's okay, Mom. Don't cry. We made it. It's going to be alright."

The mom didn't seem to be overly moved by her young boy's compassion, but I was. Because in that simple gesture of touching her mom's arm and in the words of solace he offered to her, this kid knew what was important at that moment. More than getting to his seat and getting buckled in, more than getting his stuff put where it had to go, the boy knew what mattered at that moment—reassuring his mom, flustered with anxiety and worry, that things would be fine.

In my anxiety about getting home on time and worrying about whether my flights would make it, this kid put everything into the proper perspective for me—reaching out and loving others is perhaps the most important calling we have.

That's what truly matters.

The world is getting busier and has been for some time. And it's not going to slow down. Technology and our ability to cram more and more into our days means there are fewer forces mandating us to slow down. And in this quickened pace, we are all faced with making decisions about what matters.

Jesus offers us a lesson today from Matthew 15 on what matters. At that time, there were all kinds of Jewish laws that dictated one's degree of holiness. A careful, meticulous reading of the Old Testament will reveal many rules and regulations that dictated whether one was defiling themselves in the eyes of God.

Jesus comes along, of course, and turns this thinking on its head. What matters in the eyes of God is not whether one eats with unwashed hands or violates all those other persnickety rules. What matters is what comes out of one's heart—how we treat others.

This is what we should be concerned about because it reflects one's commitment to following in the ways of God. And when these questions get buried beneath issues of how one eats and what one eats and whether this touches that and so on, we lose perspective on what truly matters. We set aside holiness for rule-following.

We're all guilty of this lifestyle from time to time. We all measure our place in life and in the eyes of others by our level of busyness or who we know or the possessions we acquire. We judge our kids' success strictly by the results of their school work or the number of extracurricular activities they excel in, instead of by the meaningful relationships they have and the ways they give of themselves to others.

What matters is how we respond to the grace of Jesus Christ by doing the right thing—by living in ways that would please God: honesty, faithfulness, kindness, and enhancing the lives of others.

In the church, we all can be guilty of the same kind of wrongful prioritizing. If we're not careful, we can let the wrong criteria rise to the top when making decisions about what we should do and who we should include in our work.

What matters when it comes to who we include in the life of the church? Based upon Jesus' dismissal of unwashed hands as something that would defile, it seems he would dismiss the criteria we often use to keep people out of the church's life.

Jesus says it really shouldn't matter what you wear when you come to church. (Now, if you show up in your bathing suit for worship and you're not on your way to the pool, yeah that might be a problem; but other than that, your dress shouldn't dictate your inclusion.)

And the same is true of your background. It shouldn't matter whether you're from Nebraska or Tennessee or any point in between. You're welcome in the church. It shouldn't matter what you look like or how much money you have. It shouldn't matter your sexual orientation, your level of education, or the neighborhood in which you live. It shouldn't matter if you're a life-long member of the church, a brand-new member, or a member who got mad at the church, left, and now feels pulled to come back.

What matters is one's commitment to living lives graced by God and fueled by an urging to love and serve others. What matters is where one's heart is.

If you paid attention at all to the news this week, you couldn't help but learn of the death of comedian Robin Williams. As much of a comedic talent as he was, his suicide this week left the world struggling to come up with an explanation for why he took his life. And it left us again with the sad reality that depression and addiction are mighty, mighty forces that even the most successful struggle to overcome.

Anne Lamotte is a person of faith and author. And on her blog this week, she wrote about Williams' death and offered some helpful words for all of us.

"There is no meaning in Robin's death, except as it sheds light on our common humanity, as his life did. But I've learned that there can be meaning without things making sense.

"Here is what is true: a third of the people you adore and admire in the world and in your families have severe mental illness and/or addiction. I sure do. I have both. And you still love me. You help hold me up. I try to help hold you up. Half of the people I love most have both; and so do most of the artists who have changed and redeemed me, given me life. Most of us are still here, healing slowly and imperfectly. Some days are way too long.

"And I hate that, I want to say. I would much prefer that God have a magic wand, and not just a raggedy love army of helpers. Mr. Rogers' mother told him when he was a boy, and a tragedy was unfolding that seemed to defy meaning, 'Look to the helpers.' That is the secret of life, for Robin's family, for you and me."

What matters is being part of the army of helpers that Mr. Rogers talked about, looking out for and helping those who are fighting illnesses they cannot fight on their own.

That's what the Holy Spirit created the church to be: an army of helpers. That's why we are together, and this is who we will be together. Amid confusion and not having any answers to the tragedy around us, we will be the hands and feet of Christ—no matter where we've come from, what we look like, or what we have.

More than the minutia we get so wrapped up in, more than questions of status, busyness, or etiquette, this is what truly matters: that which comes from our hearts.

Fundamental Neighborliness
Luke 16:19-31

In the neighborhood we live in, there are two houses that stand out. One is a huge mansion-type residence that dwarfs all the other houses in size and opulence. It's the house everyone who moves into the subdivision wants to take their friends or family to see after they've moved in. We do so because we know we'd never be able to afford such a place ourselves and like to dream for a moment that we could, or because we just like to marvel at its gaudy dimensions.

This home is tucked away in the back of the subdivision. You don't go by it unless you make the effort to; it doesn't get passed on your way home.

The second house that stands out in the neighborhood is one that you can't help but see. Virtually everyone who lives in the subdivision must go by it as they come and go.

It is the opposite of the first house. Unlike the first home, it is moderate in size. But it doesn't generate much desire to look at it twice. It's plain and comes across as somewhat broken down. Its lawn isn't cared for like the others in the neighborhood. More than anything else, it has had a revolving door when it comes to who has lived in the house over the years.

It's a rental home, and people have moved in and out regularly over the last decade.

If people who lived in the subdivision answered honestly, we'd probably tell you we don't want to know what goes on at that house. We want to shield our eyes from it as we go by, but we look at it anyway for further proof that it just doesn't measure up to our neighborhood's standards.

There are some folks who live nearby who have taken an interest in the house and its residents. John and Betty live just a few doors down, and Betty especially is a very welcoming neighbor. As soon as somebody new moves in, Betty goes down to welcome them and invite them to our neighborhood gatherings.

Once we've met the residents there, we find them to be very nice, gracious, and interested in being good neighbors themselves.

They may have somewhat chaotic family dynamics, but most have been eager to live lives that are quiet, normal, and noble.

Why don't we do more for the residents in this house who most likely don't have the financial assets others around them have or run around in the same social circles we do? Why don't we reach out to them and help them assimilate better into the neighborhood or the community?

Fundamental neighborliness involves showing the same love and compassion to those different from us in social or economic standing.

As the parable of the rich man and Lazarus points out today, it is to this population that showing fundamental neighborliness takes priority.

These are not two similar people that Jesus compares in this tale. The one lying outside the gates is a poor, homeless, hungry man, while the one inside the gates is rich and lives a life of comfort.

When they both die, however, and the rich man finds himself in hell begging for someone to cool his tongue from the fire, Abraham, the gate keeper there, basically says it's too late for him. He didn't repent of his ways before his death—ways that involved keeping all his money and turning a blind eye to those in need around him (most notably Lazarus).

The rich man resigns himself to his fate but tries to get Lazarus to go to his five brothers and tell them what they must do to avoid a similar sentence. Abraham says to him, though, "They have Moses and the prophets; they should listen to them."

In other words, for his living brothers, they still had time to heed God's word—a word that makes a strong preference for the poor and the need to be neighborly to them.

What is the single-most important command we as people of faith should heed? Is it truly to believe in Jesus Christ so that our sins are forgiven and that we might be granted eternal life? That would seem to be the obvious answer.

No doubt it's important. But Jesus spoke of the need to love our neighbors as much as he spoke of the need to love him. And the neighbors he had in mind were never the ones who seemed to have everything going for them. They were like Lazarus, the ones we always seem to want to shade our eyes from. They are different from us, maybe even eyesores.

Fundamental neighborliness is about what we do for those who have less food or lesser housing or lesser education or whose pasts are less sterling. The Lazaruses of our day may not literally be outside our fences begging for food; but they aren't far away.

Our neighbors are the poor and homeless, but our neighbors are also those who we think have it all together but are spiritually poor. It's the person who, amid difficult times, longs for somebody to care. When they are feeling lonely, there is nothing like a phone call from a friend, just to say "hello" or, "Are you okay?" And, of course they're not okay, but the simple fact that someone took notice of them and asked can lift their spirits.

We've all been there, and we all know how wonderful it is simply to be noticed when our world is caving in around us.

When have we last called a lonely friend or checked up on a depressed neighbor? Do we offer a bottle of water to the drunkard slouched against the wall, or do we step to the other side of the street to avoid him? Do we see Lazarus sitting right at our gate, or do we just walk by him day in and day out, no more noticing him than the bush adorning the other side of the driveway?

In this parable today, Jesus is saying in effect, "You've heard it from Moses. You've heard it from the prophets. You've heard it from me…a bunch! If you are going to follow me, you must help the people in need. You must feed the hungry and clothe the naked. You must help the widow and the orphan. You must offer shelter to the homeless and comfort to the grieving. You must visit the imprisoned and offer forgiveness to those who have wronged you. And to do any of that means you start by noticing the need of the people around you!"

The question can be asked: "Who is our neighbor?" Are our eyes open to the neighbors around us who, like Lazarus, are right outside our gates and who could never be mistaken for a person who has enough? Or maybe we need to look a little more closely to see the neighbors who might have enough to feed their stomachs but instead are hungry for nourishment to feed their spirits.

For as long as we have breath in this life, we have the opportunity to be good neighbors—driven by the desire that all in body and spirit would one day have enough.

Tilting Our Ears
Psalm 78:1-4

A week ago Friday night, I was driving home after dropping our son Jacob off at an event at the John Knox Center. It was about 7:30, and I had turned the radio on to a local station that was broadcasting a local high school football game. Bearden High was the visiting team. And the announcers began the broadcast by announcing that Bearden would be without its starting kicker for the game.

And of course, when you hear of a starter not playing, you think of an injury that must have occurred. Or you think of a suspension for poor grades or other off-the-field conduct.

But, no, the announcer said that the starting kicker would be missing the game that night because…he had forgotten to bring his kicking shoes with him to the game.

That's the first time I had ever heard that announced in public. It's probably happened many times with young kids. But it's the first time I had heard on a radio broadcast that an important player on an athletic team would not be playing because he had forgotten a key piece of his uniform back home.

The announcer then said that, while there had been time to make other arrangements to get the young man some shoes, the coach and the parents had elected not to do so as a way of teaching the young man a lesson about responsibility and paying attention to detail.

Immediately, I sympathized with the boy and his parents. As the parent of two young boys, I know what it's like to be taking your kid to a tennis lesson, for example, and then realize your kid has forgotten his tennis racket. And then, when this happens, you remember your own days as a kid and the lack of focus you had that resulted in some sort of embarrassing experience.

Incidents like this happen because we are usually tuned out to what is essential at a particular moment. When this young football player was packing his stuff for the game that afternoon, he no doubt knew he had to pack his shoes. But his mind's attention was captured by something else at the moment. Maybe he had been dreaming of kicking the game-winning field goal, or maybe he was dreaming of his girlfriend running into his arms later that night after he had made the game-winning field goal.

No matter, his mind was elsewhere—away from the pertinent task at hand.

It happens too often to all of us. Call it absent-mindedness, call it being scatter brained, or call it simple forgetfulness. Whatever. When our minds drift away from what is most important at the time, it can lead to some disappointing results.

The comparison can be made to those moments when we aren't in synch with what God would have us do, with what God's intentions are for that moment.

The psalmist implores his listeners to incline their ears toward his teaching about all the wonders God has done. The Common English Bible translates this phrase in verse 1 as, "Tilt your ears to the words of my mouth."

If we tilt our ears, we're in tune with teachings that reflect the goodness of God—all of the blessings God has made.

Today, with talk of war in Syria and Iraq once again, with talk of an economy that just can't seem to get out of its own way, with talk of racial problems that continue to dog our society, with talk of income inequality and a shrinking middle class, it is tempting for our ears to get tilted away from the reality of God's blessings. It is tempting to get distracted by teachings that would instruct us on the decline and impending doom of the world.

The psalmist says, though, tilt your ears this way. Tilt your ears toward the greatness of God. When we do, we can better see a glass that is half full rather than half empty.

New York Times columnist David Brooks wrote a column this past week that seems out of the mainstream. Held up against the news of the day, it seems illogical. And yet, it might just be ideas to which we might tilt our ears. The title of his column is "Snap Out of It."

"The scope of the problems we face are way below historic averages. We face nothing like the slavery fights of the 1860s, the brutality of child labor and industrialization of the 1880s, or a civilization-threatening crisis like World War I, the Great Depression, World War II or the Cold War. Even next to the 1970s — which witnessed Watergate, stagflation, social decay and rising crime — we are living in a golden age."

Is Brooks right? Is this really a golden age for our nation? A daily dose of the evening news, a daily tilting of our ears in that direction, would indicate not. But we need to make a judgment as to who or what we focus on. We shouldn't get distracted so that we lose focus on the big picture. The big picture for David Brooks was the overall prosperity he sees around the world.

For people of faith, the big picture, echoed by the psalmist, is that we have much to be thankful for. We have a God who has done wondrous works. We have a God who, according to the writer later in this Psalm, has led God's people out of Egypt, split the sea and led them through, led them with a cloud by day and lightning through the night, split rocks open in the wilderness and made streams flow so they had water to drink.

In the face of considerable challenge, the psalmist was a glass half-full guy—all because he firmly believed in clinging to the God who brings good news.

At some point, all of us for our own sanity and for the sake of gaining the proper perspective must turn off the news that seems to be riddled with complaint. At some point, we all must tilt our ears away from the person or people in our lives who can only find the worst of our society to talk about. At some point, we all must suspend our worrying about security, morality, and a declining standard of living and focus our attention on all the wonderful works God has done.

Those works are revealed through the Bible, but they are also revealed in the countless people we meet every day.

Who tilts your ears toward God's wondrous works? We can define pretty easily who tilts our ears away from the Good News. Who draws you toward it and keeps you there?

This week, I was saddened to hear of the death of a man to whom I tilted my ears often since I graduated from seminary. His name was Tom Jorgenson, and he served as the chairman of the Pastor Nominating Committee that called me to serve as the associate pastor at the First Presbyterian Church in Hastings, Nebraska, in 1999.

Tom was the biggest cheerleader of that church, that city, and Hastings College that one could find. He was jovial, caring, and committed. And he was God's mouthpiece fifteen years ago when he was adamant in convincing me that Hastings was where I should begin my ministry. And during my three years there and in recent years until he became ill, my ears always tilted toward him when looking for a smile or encouragement, or a reminder of the importance of friendships.

Tilt your ears to voices like that.

And if you can't think of anybody, think of Jesus. Think of a man who gave of his life for all, who came alongside those who were outcast and thought they had no chance at being loved. Think of a guy who puts aside all the ugly behaviors we demonstrate and forgives us.

Christ and those who represent Christ to us need to have our focus. Without them, we might end up in situations or in places that may not bring out our best or help us find our greatest joy.

In which direction are our ears titled today?

Triggers of the Holy
John 21:1-14

In Bellevue where we live and up until this year, there was a familiar sound that we would hear in the afternoons of the fourth week of August. Airplanes would be circling above. These were not jetliners, nor were they single engine crop dusters. No, these airplanes produced a special roar that truly got your attention.

They were fighter jets. And whenever we heard them, we wouldn't get concerned that war had broken out and the Air Force had been called into action. No, upon hearing the deafening sound of the fighter jets overhead during that week, we suddenly would be reminded that it was air show week at Offutt Air Force Base, which is just blocks from the church I serve.

The planes would be practicing for the maneuvers and stunts they'd perform at the two-day event on the base that attracted thousands of spectators each year. We locals, while tiring a bit of the noise by the end of the week, came to realize that the planes practicing up above triggered the approaching arrival of a long-running community event.

Like the roar of the jets overhead, there are many sounds, smells, and pictures that trigger memories or an awareness of an event taking place.

The sight of cars at a dead stop on the interstate a few hundred yards in front of us trigger the recognition of an accident that has occurred and that arrival at our destination will be delayed.

Or, the sound of two five-year-old feet hitting the floor above us in our home lets Jenni and me know that soon we will be graced with the presence of a child who is still up way too late or who has awakened far too early.

When these things happen, we can't help but recognize our surroundings or be taken back into our memories.

The seasons of the year certainly serve as triggers, too. The first sight of green in our yards triggers spring's approach. The first start of the air conditioner triggers the warmth of summer, the first turning of the leaves triggers the crispness of autumn, and the first frost on the ground triggers the coming of winter.

For people of faith, the turning of the church calendar, too, makes us aware of the significant events that have shaped us.

This past Spring, on the day before Easter, our five-year-old son, Joey, and I were sitting at the kitchen table early in the morning mapping out the Saturday in front of us. I had agreed to take him to a movie later in the day, which he was excited about. But before that, I said, we have to go to the church for the Easter Egg-stravaganza.

"Oohh," he said. "What will we do there?"

"Well, there will be an inflatable bounce house." And his eyes lit up.

"And there's going to be a piñata for the kids to swing at." His eyes got a little bigger.

"And," I said, "there's going to be an Easter egg hunt."

And Joey's eyes got even bigger and suddenly he shouted, "Christ is risen!"

For this five-year-old preacher's kid, it's the search for plastic eggs with chocolate inside that triggers recognition of the risen Christ.

The text from John 21 today contains moments of recognition—moments when these ordinary people, based on something they saw happen, triggered clear awareness of Christ's presence.

On two different occasions, a fascinating event occurred that, based on the disciples' knowledge of who could've been responsible, signaled a resounding affirmation of God's nearness.

The disciples, struggling to find the right place on the water where the nets would garner a catch, succumb to the instructions of a guy standing on the shore and redirect their nets to the other side of the boat. And when these nets come up this time, they are full of fish.

That seemingly rich harvest is the unmistakable work of Jesus, so says one of the disciples.

When they had all come ashore, they found a fire going with fish cooking on it and some bread. The disciples are invited by the host to sit and have breakfast. And upon hearing that invitation, the disciples didn't have to bother to ask who he was. His invitation to them to share in the bountiful meal was all the proof they needed of Jesus' presence.

In both encounters, Jesus' identity was triggered not by self-identifying words but by the gifts he brought them--gifts that were relevant to their own particular lives at that particular moment: fish to make a living and breakfast to feed their hungry stomachs.

In the sea of Tiberius, if anybody was going to know where the fish were, it should have been the disciples. Fishing there was their livelihood. So, when the guy standing on the shore tells them to throw the nets on the other side of the boat and they find a bonanza, it could have meant only one thing.

And when they are later offered breakfast on the shore, this host's invitation to them to share in the meal he had provided instantly revealed who he was. "Come and eat," he said to them. They had heard those words before.

They recognized the risen Christ because he revealed himself in ways that were unique to them and left them no doubt.

There are moments in our own lives when we have little doubt that Christ is near. And those moments come in the people we meet or the places we visit—people and places that are unique to the joys we find and the challenges we face.

I would imagine that for those of you who worship in this space on a regular basis, simply entering this sanctuary triggers the presence of a God who is vast, mighty, and victorious. This space would seem to leave no doubt about that. And it left no doubt in me each time I entered it when I served with you as one of your pastors. It's an awe-inspiring space.

By the same token, we also experience triggers that reveal God's intimacy and personal love for us: the children or grandchildren who tells us they love us; the phone message from a kid we've mentored—who once betrayed our trust but who now expresses how much he needs us in his life and wants an opportunity to make things right; or the person who, in the midst of a down day we're having, takes the time to pop in and thank us for something we didn't realize meant so much to him or her.

These people, these events, and these places reveal the living God.

As we cherish those moments when Christ makes himself known, we should remember that God uses us as triggers so that others might have the living Lord revealed to them. We are the vessels by which God becomes known to the world.

Rev. Gary D. Jones is rector of St. Stephens Episcopal Church in Richmond, Virginia. In a recent article he wrote for a newsletter called *Spirit*, he shared his experience at a clinic where he himself had been treated for cancer.

"Not long ago, I had to return to the clinic where I had been treated between my hospitalizations for an aggressive cancer. The clinic was the place where I went to have my blood drawn and analyzed, just to make sure the chemotherapy wasn't killing me. Those visits were hard, and I wasn't eager to return. All the way there, I was dreading it.

"And when I arrived, I saw it was all pretty much the same – lots of bald people waiting to have their blood drawn or to receive a blood transfusion. Some with family members, others waiting alone, and a few with a kind of vacant look in their eyes. 'How did I get here?' they seemed to be thinking. 'I'm going to die soon anyway; maybe I should just go home. But I'm afraid. Nobody knows what this is really like…if only somebody would hold me and love me….'

"And then I noticed the sweet nurses who had played such an important role in my healing. I had hair now, so they didn't recognize me. But they were still going up to the gaunt patients in the waiting room, smiling and calling the patients by name, putting their arms around these people who could hardly walk. '*Come unto me*,' Jesus said, '*all you who are weary and carrying heavy burdens, and I will give you rest.*' This is exactly what the nurses were saying, in their gentle, loving and encouraging way.

"And then, I heard a nurse inside an adjacent room, flipping through charts, as she prepared to call her next patient. "Gary Jones," she said quietly and reflectively to herself. And then, as if suddenly remembering, she burst out loudly, 'GARY JONES!' and came running out of the room to where I was sitting. At first, she didn't recognize me, because she had never seen me with hair. And besides, I had started weeping when I heard her calling my name. I don't know what happened to me; I just couldn't help it.

"But I recognized her. She had cared for me for months. She was my sister, my mother, my friend, my priest…. In the way that Jesus intended us to be for each other, I realized that she was my Lord, whom I recognized when she called my name."

We are that nurse, we are the friend who listens, we are the teacher, the coach, the mentor, the care-giver. We are the triggers by which others know that Christ is alive.

Having a Little Faith
Luke 17:5-10

Last week in our focus on the parable of the rich man and Lazarus, I referenced the Grand Canyon as a metaphor for the great chasm between where we are as the rich of the world (relatively speaking) and the place we are called to get to regarding serving the poor. It seems an unlikely transition for us, but with God's help we can still cross this great divide and find ourselves in the place we want to be.

Today, the Grand Canyon sounds like a good metaphor again. Except, this time, the great distance of the canyon feels like the chasm between the amount of faith we have and the amount of faith we think we should have. Much like the canyon is awesome and a seemingly impossible distance to cross, the gap between where we are in our faith and where we seem pressured to be can also seem too great.

All of us have grand plans to take big leaps of faith—to reach places of faith we see others occupying. We can't help but view these folks as mentors and examples of what it truly means to be the disciples Jesus time after time calls us to be. We see their great diligence in prayer, study, or service, and we dream of having that same fervent and robust faith.

But after a while, despite our best effort, we just don't think we can ever fully get there—ever fully answer the call God has placed on our lives.

We become consumed with wanting to take big strides, but our gate simply isn't that long.

This is true also of the success we envision for ourselves in the careers we've chosen. We have or had dreams of being the CEO, but we can't or couldn't get out of the entry level. We want to be the principal of the school but we're still teaching in the classroom. We aspire to become the police chief but still remain on the night patrol.

We want to take big leaps, but our stride simply isn't that long.

Parker Palmer is a Christian writer. In a lecture he delivered to other writers and people of faith a few years ago at Calvin College, he reminded his audience that another strategy is best employed if we want to realize our dreams. It's a strategy that is based on small steps—baby steps even—instead of big leaps.

Palmer talked about the struggles and frustrations he experienced over many years in his journey to become a successful writer. He had dreams of getting published—writing books being his ultimate goal. But when it seemed like he was just spinning his wheels to get started, he became quite frustrated.

One day, he came across a line that was once written by Hemmingway, a line that helped put into perspective the value of the journey in getting us to the desired outcomes.

"A writer," Hemmingway said, "is distinguished by the fact that he writes." It wasn't until he read this line from Hemingway that he was able to approach the challenge of writing with freshness and confidence. This sentence unleashed in Palmer the understanding that it's the faithful *doing* of the thing, the willingness to work hard at the craft without worrying too much about outcomes, that makes you a writer.

It seems the act of becoming the people of faith God imagines us to be is similar to the approach we should take in becoming CEOs or principals or police chiefs…or successful parents or supervisors or spouses or Cub Scout leaders or anything we aspire to become. It takes baby steps—several of them, hundreds of them, thousands of them. Most of the time, we're incapable of giant leaps. Rarely is it possible to go from spiritual novice to seasoned disciple overnight.

Most of the time, it takes a lifetime of baby steps to get to the destination God intends for us to reach.

In Luke 17, Jesus lays out the requirements for the disciples being able to uproot and plant a mulberry tree into the sea. To accomplish that spectacular feat, Jesus did not say they had to have faith the size of a tornado or hurricane or a volcano. No, they needed faith the size of a mustard seed.

You must look quite hard to see a mustard seed. It's as tiny as seeds come. Overnight, it won't grow into a large and thriving plant. It takes time and patient nurturing for a mustard seed to grow into its intended result.

Jesus wanted the disciples to know that to do great things for the kingdom of God required not huge leaps of faith by one person, but thousands of baby steps each day by all believers. Much like a servant doing daily chores for a master, we all have small jobs to do to ensure that our Master is properly served.

Like a servant coming in after a hard day's work and doing his duty by serving dinner to his master, we simply do our duty. If we are writers, we write; if we are teachers, we teach. If we are doctors, we treat patients; if we are engineers, we, well, I have no idea what engineers do (but it's important).

We do our jobs; that's all. As Christians, we do our jobs—loving, teaching, worshiping, welcoming. Those are our jobs. And it's all we need to do.

In the last several weeks, we've read some of the texts in Luke and maybe have been intimidated by the demands Jesus places upon us. There was this great call to help the poor, to serve God and not wealth, and the strange call to hate one's family in order to be a disciple.

The bar was set high by Jesus in these stories.

Today, instead of being challenged, we find comfort from Jesus. The only faith we need is that of the size of a mustard seed. It need not be huge. Mustard seed-size faith is enough. Doing our duty, doing our jobs is enough.

A small thing we can do today or in the coming days is contribute to the Peace and Global Witness offering. If we all contributed something small, the offering's impact would be great in restoring the lives of young people.

Or we can go on the Hunger Hike today at Victor Ashe Park to raise money to fight hunger in our community. Hundreds of folks today will be taking little steps to have a big impact on our community.

But having just a little faith isn't only about what we *do*. It is also about what we think and believe. And who among us hasn't claimed to have only a little faith in God when tough times strike. When that cancer diagnosis comes, when that spouse has died leaving you all alone, when that assortment of failed financial deals all seem to hit at the same time, when just stepping outside is difficult for fear of gun violence or bombs that would injure or kill—in these moments, it is difficult to be a pillar of faith.

On this World Communion Sunday, I think about the Church in different places around the world. I think about the church in Aleppo, the Syrian being destroyed by war. What is the level of Christians' faith in Aleppo this morning? Are they in the spirit of breaking the bread and drinking the cup this morning? Are they even capable of worshiping this morning?

What about Christians in places like Iraq and Afghanistan, where Islamic terrorists are torturing and killing Christians? What does their communion table look like today? Are people hopeful enough to come to the table?

In these places where it is hard to have faith at all, Jesus would say to these brothers and sisters that faith the size of a mustard seed is enough. In your heartbreak and in your fear, God's grace is for you as much as it is for anybody. Just a little faith will do.

If you feel you're only spinning your wheels and aren't making any progress to get where God intends for you to be, or if you clearly think you're on the way, take a few steps—small as they may be. Our collective steps will make a difference in the lives of those we serve.

Again, Parker Palmer, the author who stressed the importance of taking small steps toward becoming the writer he wanted to become, paralleled his journey to the journey of faith. He said, "The faith journey is less about making a big leap of faith than it is about putting one faithless foot in front of the other, and doing it again and again."

The faith of a mustard seed—small but committed—is all we need.

At Your Service
Mark 10:46-52

Radio talk show hosts are a rare breed. First, there aren't many of them compared to the rest of the population. It only seems like they are everywhere.

Second, radio talk show hosts (especially the ones who give advice to people seeking cures for their problems) need to be able to blend a certain expertise with a high ability to articulate that expertise and a refined ability to listen well.

They also need to know how to move things along on the radio when the conversation seems to be getting bogged down. People who call into radio shows, you see, tend to not have all the traits of a good radio host. Not all of them have the skill to be succinct and coherent in their questions.

Many a time must a host move the conversation along and get to the real crux of a long, rambling phone call. One of the tactics I've heard hosts use is a sudden, interruptive question: "So how can I help you today?" It helps the caller to quickly summarize and get to his or her query.

Yes, they want to know how they can help, but they really just want to move things along.

In this account from Mark 10, Jesus, too, may be wanting to move a conversation along; but most likely, he's more interested in knowing what a blind man truly wants from him in that moment.

Consider this story of Bartimaeus, the blind beggar seated on the side of the road in Jericho. He knew that Jesus was near, and he kept shouting at the top of his lungs, "Son of David, have mercy on me!" Now, if you or I were walking down Kingston Pike and encountered a blind guy begging for food or money and shouting at the top of his lungs something about God having mercy on him, I'm not sure we would rush to his aid. In fact, we would most likely look with disdain on the guy, assuming his past had to be very checkered, that he had had enough chances, and that another handout from anybody who would pass by would be a foolish waste of one's time and money.

Jesus, as we might expect, doesn't subscribe to that line of reasoning. He beckons Bartimaeus to come to him. And when he's in front of him, Jesus doesn't assume what his needs are and doesn't give him something he doesn't need. No, he takes time to ask with all genuineness and sincerity: "What do you want me to do for you?"

And with that simple question, we have reinforced to us another piece of God's identity. Not only is God the omnipotent creator of the universe, God is concerned about what each of our needs are and wants us to tell God what those needs are.

You'd expect an all-knowing, all-powerful God to already know what's troubling Bartimaeus. And if God already knows what the issues are, you'd expect Jesus to simply grant the healing he already knows Bartimaeus seeks.

But, no, Jesus asks first. "What do you want me to do for you?"

What can I do? How can I help you? How can I be of service? Those are all different versions of the same kind of approach Jesus takes with Bartimaeus. He's there to help, but he also is interested in hearing from Bartimaeus himself what he would like to see done.

How many of us, when speaking with a customer service representative of some business on the telephone hasn't been on the receiving end of such phrases? And how many of us, when hearing those phrases, have questioned whether the person asking the question is sincere in what he or she is asking?

After waiting on hold for 10 minutes, you get that predictable opening line: "Hi, my name is Dave. How may I help you today?" And immediately you question whether Dave is in the mood for helping you.

Or, at the end of one of these phone calls, you're finally eager to get off the phone, but the customer service rep won't let you off. There's a string of comments designed to make you feel good about the business you've just gotten through arguing with. But, they only leave you more frustrated. You're ready to hang up and Dave says, "Is there anything else I can help you with today, Mr. Nieman?"

It's often not just the words that people choose to make you feel they care, it's how they say them.

We weren't privy to Jesus' body language and voice inflections when he asked Bartimaeus, "What do you want me to do for you?" But, judging from the fact that he stopped when he didn't have to stop, that he wasn't getting paid by anybody to help

Bartimaeus, and based upon his compassion that he had shown to others in the past, he probably didn't come across as being put up to this task by his heavenly father or anyone else.

He honestly wanted to know, "How can I help you today?"

That question is reflective of Jesus' nature as the great high priest that the writer of Hebrews talks about. Priests in that day were the ones known to be the intermediaries between God and humanity. They still are. They were the ones called by God to ask these questions of the people in honest and sincere ways.

But, this priest, as the writer of Hebrews points out, is different. He is the one who is holy, blameless, undefiled, and who has been made perfect forever. He is the one sent by God to be the ultimate intermediary between God and humanity.

He is the one who is at our service asking, "What do you want me to do for you?"

Jesus, the servant leader.

If there's a mistake we make during the difficult steps along our life's journeys, it's that we believe God isn't interested in hearing from us what's on our minds. We don't take seriously the fact that Jesus wants to know from us what it is that God can do for us. It doesn't matter if we're right or wrong in our thanksgivings, intercessions, or laments. What's important is that God wants to know. God wants to hear it from our own mouths and hearts.

If you've ever sensed that your spouse or your kids are troubled by something and have attempted to have a dialogue with them about it, you've probably gotten a predictable response when you inquire. They say, "Oh, nothing." It's the silent treatment at its best.

"Are you sure there isn't something bothering you?"

"Yeah."

"Promise?"

"Yeah."

All the while, you know something is on their minds. You want to help, but they aren't ready to allow you to help.

God stands willing and ready to be an agent of assistance and comfort, if only we ask.

And that asking can come simply. It can come through the power of prayer—either in a formal, worshipful setting such as this—or in the quiet isolation of any number of places where we find ourselves.

"God, help me be stronger today as I face the lure of temptation."

"God, take away the pain of my mother who is about at her breaking point."

"God, rescue the world from the pit of violence and war."

"God, I'm lonely and alone and have no one to turn to."

"God, protect my child. Help him to not hurt himself or anybody else."

God invites us to share, repeatedly even, what is most on our hearts.

By the same token, our calling as God's children should also involve us asking the same question, "What do you want me to do for you?" As Jesus asked that of Bartimaeus, so should we be asking that of those in need around us.

That question we ask of others can do wonders for the human condition. If we would only ask it more often—to those we know and to those who are total strangers—imagine the progress that would be made toward reconciliation and unity among cultures, races, and other social groups.

"What do you want me to do for you?" Imagine what those words could mean coming from a Palestinian to an Israeli (or vice versa) in the Middle East, from a Sunni Muslim to a Shiite Muslim (or vice versa) in Iraq, from a Protestant to a Roman Catholic (or vice versa) in Northern Ireland, from a middle-class family in Farragut to a lower-income family in East Knoxville (or vice versa), or from an adult to an at-risk child in one of our schools.

Imagine the barriers broken down, the greater camaraderie established, and the lesser conflict that so often brings so much unnecessary heartache and suffering around the world.

Jesus was willing to take that step, asking the question that involved some vulnerability and courage on his part. And in doing so, he revealed another key piece of God's makeup. In the person of Jesus, God becomes personal, near to us, and willing to invest in our lives.

"What do you want me to do for you?" Bartimaeus says, "I want to see!" Jesus says, "Your faith has healed you." And Bartimaeus saw.

One simple question that changed his world.

The Hope of Any Preacher or Parent
1 Thessalonians 2:9-13

Last week, I spent 8 days at a conference called Presbyterian Credo. Credo in Latin means "belief." Similar to that is the word "creed," from which we derive statements of faith like the Apostles' Creed.

Presbyterian Credo is a conference for Presbyterian clergy to discover not so much what they believe theologically but instead who they are in areas relating to their physical, spiritual, vocational, and financial health. Sponsored by the Board of Pensions of the PCUSA, the eight-day event gives clergy a break, a time to catch their breath, to worship, and to form community with others on the same journey.

It was a wonderful week, and I thank you (especially my wife) for the time away.

When one is gone for a week, there are always things you miss out on. And so I missed parent-teacher-student conferences in the Bellevue Schools. We all know what those are. They've been part of the educational process for quite some time. Here, they are 15-minute slots of time that parents and students spend with a child's teacher. In the elementary schools, you go into the classroom, review the child's work over the first quarter of the year, and then have a conversation about what's gone well and what the student can improve upon as the year continues.

The teacher also gives the family a copy of his or her report card, which details progress in many different areas. Because I couldn't attend the conference at school, I did see Jacob's report card when I got home. Everything was in good order.

There are several different sections to consider when you open this elementary school report card. There are evaluations in the areas of language arts, math, science, social studies, health, physical education, music, and art. There's also a section on the right-hand side of the report card that always seems to get my attention first. It's the section on work habits and social skills.

It's in this section that students get graded on how well they follow instructions, listen attentively, show respect, greet others, resist peer pressure, give compliments, and assumes responsibility.

Each time Jacob has gotten a report card, my eyes drift to this section first. And I've found myself asking why. Certainly, the key to a young person's success in a global economy over the next two decades will be determined largely by how talented one is in math, science, and language arts. These are the crucial areas that will determine success.

Yet I can't help but first look at those areas that pertain to being a good citizen. I'm interested—supremely interested—in how well my son is treating his classmates and his teachers. I'm interested in the courtesy he displays when disagreeing with someone, when he's given a gift, when he's corrected by a teacher, or when he makes an apology.

It's the parent in me, I guess, who will always be more concerned with how he gets to where he's going rather than what that destination will be.

The apostle Paul, in what is widely believed to be his earliest writing to the early church, reminds the people of Thessalonica of his encouragement of them—of his urging and pleading that they might lead lives worthy of God.

In my concern over my son's work habits and social skills, I'm revealing my bias as a parent who longs for his son to lead a life worthy of God. That means following his call but following it in a way that brings honor to the One who created him.

We honor God by our behavior. Honor comes when we stick up for what we believe but respect the point of view of our neighbor who doesn't share our views. Honor comes when we compete as hard as we can but at the end of the day—win or lose—congratulate our opponent on their good effort.

A couple of weeks ago in the National Football League, the head coaches of opposing teams starting shouting at each other and almost started taking swings at each other when meeting for the post-game handshake. And in the aftermath of the incident, there actually were commentators who advocated doing away with the post-game ritual of shaking hands. That way, these kinds of confrontations would be avoided.

In a world where civility is in short supply already, we need more sportsmanlike gestures rather than less. It's through acts of conciliation like shaking hands or apologizing for our mistakes where we bring honor to God.

We honor God by our behavior.

We also honor God by answering our call. The Holy Spirit of God is always at work—calling us, nudging us, pushing us toward a greater sense of faithfulness. How will we answer?

God is calling us into his own kingdom and glory. That's what Paul said to the Thessalonians and that's what God is doing to us—calling us into something that might involve some risk.

This is Grace Hartranft's first outing as a liturgist in worship, and she's doing a fine job. And as it is for everyone who enters this pulpit for the first time, it carries with it some risk. Grace might discover after today that leading worship is where her calling is. Or she may discover it is not. But she's put herself out here in front of all of us. And that's risky.

We're all faced with the prospect of exposing our shortcomings when we attempt to answer God's call. But if we don't risk, we won't move ourselves to where God wants us to be.

Laird Stewart is a retired Presbyterian pastor and was our faculty leader at the Credo conference. And on the last morning of the conference, he told us of how he'd been playing a little game with the housekeeping staff at the retreat center all week.

In each of our rooms, there was a desk. And underneath the desk was a trash basket. Each evening, Laird would pull the trash basket out from under the desk and put it beside the desk. The next morning when the housekeepers came in, they'd put it back under the desk. And later that evening, Laird would again pull it out from under and put the basket beside the desk. And the next morning, the housekeepers would put it back underneath.

And as good preachers do, Stewart showed us the parallel between the waste basket and us. We tend to want to stay underneath and out of sight from God's call. But in God's calling each of us to something more faithful, God is always pulling us out from the shadows to be seen and heard.

We honor God by answering our call.

Through our behavior and our being faithful to who God wants us to be, God is calling us into his own kingdom and glory. Paul gave thanks to God for this calling, for God has a plan for us to prosper and not to fail.

This is what leading a life worthy of God is all about. In our actions and in our response to God's amazing grace, we become who God wants us to be.

I can't think of a better wish that pastors would have for their congregations or that parents might have for their kids.

www.ingramcontent.com/pod-product-compliance
Lightning Source LLC
Chambersburg PA
CBHW072041110526
44592CB00012B/1504